THE RELUCTANT GARDENER

JOANNA SMITH

NEW HOLLAND

First published in 2006 by
New Holland Publishers (UK) Ltd
London o Cape Town o Sydney o Auckland
www.newhollandpublishers.com

Garfield House
86–88 Edgware Road
London W2 2EA
United Kingdom

80 McKenzie Street
Cape Town 8001
South Africa

14 Aquatic Drive
Frenchs Forest
NSW 2086
Australia

218 Lake Road
Northcote
Auckland
New Zealand

2 4 6 8 10 9 7 5 3 1

ISBN 1 84537 432 0

Editor: Ruth Hamilton
Design: Sue Rose
Illustrations: Coral Mula
Production: Hazel Kirkman
Editorial direction: Rosemary Wilkinson
Cover photograph: Photos Horticultural (www.photos-horticultural.com)

Reproduction by Modern Age, Hong Kong
Printed and bound by Replika Press, India

CONTENTS

CHAPTER 1

THE GREENEST FINGERS

MAN'S BEST FRIEND

Did you know that the humble earthworm is out there working for you 24 hours a day in all weathers? These invaluable creatures improve your soil structure no end while they are feeding and burrowing by increasing aeration and helping drainage, all of which means healthier plants and less work for you. Encourage them in their work by adding well-rotted manure or other organic matter to the beds, either in the form of a mulch (the least effort), or by digging it in when planting.

IN THE GREEN

Snowdrops are invaluable in the garden because they flower in the dead of winter when there's little else around to enjoy. Cadging some off a neighbour not only makes sense in thrifty terms, but also for horticultural reasons. Snowdrops do not take well if they are planted as dry bulbs; the way to succeed is to plant them 'in the green' after they have finished flowering but when they are still in leaf. Start dropping hints early while they are in flower, then a few weeks later pop round with trowel in hand and tell them their clumps will benefit from being thinned out (which is in fact true). Be sure to plant the snowdrops to the same depth in your garden when you get them home.

URN SOME RESPECT

Stone urns are the last word in understated elegance, making any garden look a million dollars, but they don't have to be expensive. Look out for reconstituted stone which is very attractive but a fraction of the cost, and choose as large an urn as you can afford. This will make a really classy centrepiece for the garden and, if it is ornamental enough, won't even require planting which means less work for you. If you do want to enhance it with a few plants, keep it simple and stick to just one variety in a single colour to let the urn speak for itself.

WATERY WELCOME

A garden pond can be a haven for wildlife, with birds bathing, insects buzzing lazily and hedgehogs coming down for a little drink, a wonderful sight to behold. More to the point, however, is that these creatures can be useful. They will happily eat their fill of slugs, or polish off a plague of aphids before breakfast. Encourage them to visit your pond by providing a shallow bank or stones at one end to provide access to the water, and foliage cover around the pond for the more timid among them.

EASY FEEDING

To save time, effort and mental energy remembering to feed your container displays, use slow-release fertilizer blocks or spikes. Insert into the pots and they will release nutrients into the compost throughout the season, doing all the work for you. Container-grown plants don't have access to the soil to get their own nutrients so they really benefit from feeding, rewarding you with a wonderful performance.

INVITATION FOR DINNER

Lacewings have a voracious appetite for aphids so they should be actively encouraged to come and feast on yours rather than those next door. Specially designed lacewing chambers are available, filled with straw which has been treated with a pheromone to attract them. Hang one up on a fence or wall in spring, then move it into a garage or shed in the autumn to protect the overwintering lacewings. Another way to encourage these little creatures is to grow the poached egg plant (*Limnanthes douglasii*), which they love for its nectar.

A COLD SNAP

Terracotta is a nice natural material that suits just about any garden or setting, from classical or formal to cottage or modern. There are plenty of terracotta pots available for a wide range of styles and budgets. Before you buy, however, check it is frostproof. Some pots and ornaments will literally crumble before your eyes in a cold snap, so save the disappointment and buy frostproof in the first place.

A SWELL IDEA

To cut down on the chore of watering containers, mix some water-retaining crystals into the compost at planting time. These crystals swell when they get wet and hold water like little reservoirs, releasing it slowly into the compost between waterings. This is especially useful for hanging baskets and small pots which are liable to dry out quickly. They can cut watering by up to a third – good news for those of us who have got better things to do.

SENSIBLE HEDGES

If you are planning a hedge, choose your hedging plants according to the time you are prepared to spend clipping them. Why make more work for yourself? Avoid at all costs fast-growing conifers such as Leyland cypress (x *Cupressocyparis leylandii*) and Lawson cypress (*Chamaecyparis lawsoniana*) which will need cutting two or three times a year. Even privet (*Ligustrum*) needs clipping over twice a year. Choose instead holly, beech, hornbeam, berberis, escallonia or forsythia, all of which make attractive hedges and only need a haircut once a year.

GIVE THE FISH A CHANCE

Keep over-vigorous pond weed under control by dragging out a third of its volume each year in the autumn, or as necessary. If it becomes too congested, it will starve out the other plants and restrict the fish, as well as looking terrible. Leave the unwanted weed on the side of the pond overnight to allow any insects, snails and newts to get back in, then discard it the next day.

GRUB ATTACK

Summer is progressing, everyone else's tubs and hanging baskets are growing rampantly but yours are stunted and weak, what's gone wrong? As long as you are feeding and watering them well, your problem may lie under the soil. Tip out a pot and examine the contents. If the roots have been eaten and there are cream-coloured grubs in the compost then you've got vine weevils, which are becoming more and more widespread. There is a biological control which can be watered onto the compost, a nematode which attacks the grubs, but other than this the only solution is to empty out the tubs and start again with fresh compost, being sure to throw away the old compost.

SUCK THEM UP

It is a good idea to collect fallen leaves in the autumn and winter as they can kill off the lawn or smaller plants in your borders, and they do make the garden look a mess – you wouldn't want to let the side down. The simplest method is with the lawnmower on a high setting. It will chop the leaves into nice little pieces and collect them up in the grass box for you. Simply tip them into black plastic sacks, pierce a few holes in them and pile them in an out-of-the-way place. A year or so later you will have humus-rich leafmould to use as a mulch or dig into the soil when you are planting.

SLUG RECYCLING

If you are plagued with slugs and snails, trap or collect them, dispatch them humanely then put them on the compost heap where they can rot down and be returned to the garden as valuable nutrients. Although this won't give you a lot of extra compost (unless you really do have a lot of slugs), it is satisfying to think they are doing your plants some good for a change.

GLAMOUR WITHOUT THE COST

Whatever job you are dreading in the garden, there's usually a tool that will make it easier. It is obviously impractical and rather expensive to buy them all, so why not hire what you need? Hire shops stock rotavators, large mowers, strimmers, hedge trimmers, cement mixers and all sorts of other invaluable equipment. That way you get to parade around with all the latest kit without having to actually buy it.

PRINCE CHARMING

There's nothing a frog enjoys more for dinner than a tender juicy slug. These are the kinds of friends every gardener needs. Encourage frogs, toads and newts to take up residence into your garden with a small natural pool, preferably close to a flower border where they can hunt for food. And make the most of the free labour.

CONTAINER PERFECTION

To keep your container displays in the number one spot every week of the year, buy a number of inserts – basic plastic pots will do – which fit snugly inside the containers. Plant the inserts up with a fantastic display for each season, then keep them waiting in the wings. As one display fades, replace it with the next, already well established and in full flower. It's not really cheating, is it?

A GOOD START

To give plants the best possible start in life, water them thoroughly at least half an hour before planting them. If the rootballs are dry when they go in, it can take weeks for any moisture to reach the plants' roots, however much you water them. Then, dig a hole twice the size of the rootball of the plant and break up the soil in the bottom of the hole to allow the plant's roots to grow into the ground more easily. Mix in plenty of organic matter such as garden compost, well-rotted manure or leafmould, then add a handful of slow-release fertilizer such as pelleted chicken manure.

DEAD CLEVER

Deadheading is a quick and easy way to make your roses flower continually right through summer. As the blooms fade, cut the stems back to a leaf joint. Make sure you cut back to flower-bearing wood, so be sure to cut beyond the leaves that have only three leaflets rather than the usual five (this is a smart bit of know-how with which to impress gardening friends). If the stems are rather straggly, don't be afraid to cut back harder to shape the bush at the same time.

SHORT BACK AND SIDES

Mound-forming hardy perennials like geraniums and alchemilla can let themselves go after they have flowered. Not only do the flowers fade, but the foliage also starts to shrivel. They really have no self respect. Take drastic action and cut off the whole plant down to the ground with shears. You will be rewarded with brand new neat clumps of fresh foliage, improving the look of the garden no end, and even perhaps some more flowers.

DON'T BE HARD ON YOURSELF

To take the work out of weeding (but sadly not all of it), wait until the soil is moist after rain. The weeds will then be much easier to pull up.

AVOID A FROZEN WASTELAND

Don't leave bedding containers bare through winter, especially those in the front garden in full view of passers-by. Be imaginative with handsome evergreen foliage (try aucuba, skimmia, ivy or conifers), winter pansies, colourful winter heathers, little snowdrops or jolly winter aconites.

DO IT YOURSELF

To keep hanging basket displays in great shape and to cut down on the time you have to spend watering, buy a self-watering hanging basket with a built-in water reservoir. These are also invaluable if you go away for the weekend. You wouldn't want to give the neighbours an excuse to poke around now would you?

A WISE CHOICE SAVES TIME

A trip to the garden centre or nursery can be a bewildering experience. You go looking for one plant to fill a gap and you end up wanting one of everything they've got. Impulse buys are never a good idea, though. If you choose a plant which is not suited to the spot you've got, it will never do well. You'll end up wasting hours trying to help it along, then you'll have to replace it anyway. Choose plants according to the conditions that suit them, taking into consideration soil type and acidity, moisture and light. They'll be healthy, happy and handsome without your help.

SLUG-FREE HOSTAS

The most foolproof method of growing perfect hostas is to plant them in containers. This allows greater control over mucus-covered marauders. Raise the pots off the ground on pot feet or pieces of tile, and wrap specially designed slug and snail tape around the pots. This forms an impenetrable barrier which they cannot cross, however determined they are.

LOOK, NO WEEDS

If you are laying an area of gravel or bark chips, be sure to cover the ground first with weed-suppressing fabric which is designed specifically for the purpose. Insert the edges into the ground to hold it in place. Lay the gravel or bark on top with the smug knowledge that you will never have to weed this patch again.

CREATURE COMFORTS

Wildlife experts encourage us to leave an area of the garden wild as a habitat for beneficial insects, amphibians, small mammals and birds. Who are we to argue? Just make sure the neighbours know why you are doing it – you don't want to be known as a slacker.

TOP IDEA

Top-dress your rock garden with a layer of stone chips or grit. Not only will it suppress weeds and retain valuable moisture in the soil, it also acts as an attractive foil for the plants. Tuck it right under the plants' foliage to keep their leaves away from any moisture in the soil. A cheap and simple, but effective, finishing touch.

THE ACID TEST

The acid test of a good gardener is whether they know the pH value of their soil. This tells them whether their soil is acid or alkaline, and therefore which plants will do well there. Buy a simple kit from a garden centre and test your soil in a number of different places. This is useful information from a gardening point of view, but also great for showing off your horticultural excellence. "Of course our pH is 6.5, what's yours?"

PATIENCE IS A VIRTUE

However desperate you are for that new acer you've seen at the garden centre, don't buy it in the summer months. Wait until autumn when the weather is cooler and the soil is moist. That way you won't have to spend hours watering it and it is more likely to establish quickly and start growing away. And you can enjoy the warm weather without the worry.

LOVELY LILIES

Lilies have it all – wonderful scents, fantastic trumpet blooms and spectacular colours. Plant them three to a tub for a failsafe summer display. Choose plump bulbs which are firm to the touch and show no signs of mould or rot. The bulbs don't cost much and they will make a magnificent show in their first year. If you don't have the energy to feed them after flowering, ready for next year, throw them away and start again next spring.

SMOKE ALERT

Take care when positioning your barbecue, and keep it away from fences and overhanging trees which could be a fire hazard. Think, too, about where the smoke is going to go. You don't want to alert the neighbours to the fact you are having a barbecue or they will all be round to cadge a sausage.

DON'T MENTION THE P WORD

Much has been written about pruning techniques, and even the thought of it instils dread into the hearts of all but the most intrepid of gardeners. Although it is important to do it at the right time, your technique may be less crucial. Bushy shrubs such as lavender, santolina and potentilla can be pruned with shears. Simply shear off the top growth in early spring to within about 2.5 cm (1 in) of the previous year's growth. This sloppy technique even works on miniature and patio roses.

STOP THE MASSACRE

Don't kill every creepy-crawly in the garden. Not all insects are pests. Many are allies in the war against plant problems. For example, ladybird larvae eat aphids in enormous numbers, and bees help to pollinate fruit trees and other flowers. Use insecticides carefully and only when you think it is absolutely necessary.

REFRESH YOUR HONEYSUCKLE

If your honeysuckle has become a tangled mess of twiggy bare stems with fresh foliage on the outside only, you need to be assertive. In late winter or early spring, cut the whole lot off to within 60 cm (2 ft) of the ground. Fork some granular feed (fertilizer) into the soil around the base and water well. The plant will send up vigorous new growth a few weeks later and look all the better for it.

CLEMATIS COLLAPSE

Clematis wilt is a horrible disease affecting – no surprises here – clematis. Once it is infected, the plant will affect a dramatic swoon, then simply collapse and die. One way to save your plants is to plant them deep – if wilt does strike, the plant is much more likely to reshoot from the base. Plant new plants with the top of the compost 10 cm (4 in) below the soil surface. Don't forget that clematis like a cool root run, so try to plant them with their roots in the shade but their foliage in the sun.

GO SOLAR

Laying electrical cables for pond pumps, fountains and pool lights can be expensive, disruptive and lots of work – three good reasons why a reluctant gardener won't want to embark on it. Look out, instead, for solar-powered models which don't require any cables. They may not be quite as powerful as mains-powered devices but they aren't bad at all. They are also safe and convenient.

PRIZE RHODODENDRONS

If you have always been dying to grow prize rhododendrons or camellias, but have alkaline soil, invest in some large tubs and fill them with ericaceous compost (great for acid-loving plants). It is nearly impossible, not to mention time-consuming, to change the acidity of garden soil so you are better off putting them in tubs or raised beds where you can control conditions more easily.

GHASTLY GREEN

Ponds have a habit of turning green the minute you invite someone over for tea. To avoid social disgrace, plant a waterlily. The floating leaves will help to shade the water and discourage the growth of algae. Oxygenating plants, such as *Lagarosiphon major* (also known as *Elodea crispa*) and parrot feather (*Myriophyllum aquaticum*), can also help: not only do they also create shade but they will absorb minerals and carbon dioxide which will starve out algae. Keep nitrogen levels low by removing dead and decaying foliage and avoiding a build-up of fish food.

CHAPTER 2

THE MOST ABUNDANT BORDERS

DISASTER AVERTED

Roses make a spectacular show when in full bloom at the height of summer, but the effect is somewhat ruined if the leaves develop black patches or mildew, shrivel and drop off. To save the shame of it all and keep your self-respect, choose varieties which are naturally resistant to diseases, such as 'Graham Thomas'. Even so, if you notice black spots appearing on the leaves or a powdery mildew forming, spray with a special rose fungicide to nip it in the bud.

EDGING AHEAD

If you want your borders to be the envy of the street, think border edgings. An edging will introduce some structure to a flowerbed and set off your plants to perfection. There are plenty of choices, each creating a different style. Low clipped box hedges are the classic choice but also the most labour intensive. Better options include a line of closely planted chives, compact thyme plants, silvery artemisia, lavender or catmint (*Nepeta*). There are also plenty of non-living edgings which require no maintenance at all, made from woven wicker, ornate cast iron, decorative plastic or even shaped lead sheeting.

DAZZLING DAISIES

For sheer flower power in the border, plant a few osteospermums. These bushy little sub-shrubs produce countless large and exotic daisy blooms throughout the summer months and come in a wide range of bright colours from yellow, white and cream to brilliant magenta. One of the most unusual is 'Whirligig' which has white flowers with slate-blue centres and backs. The petals are shaped like spoons, giving the appearance of suckers on a frog's feet. Buy small plants from a garden centre and if you live in a frost-prone area, treat them as annuals.

DROUGHT BUSTERS

One of the key principles of a reluctant gardener is to choose plants which look after themselves (the same goes for spouses). Summer watering is a thankless task, and a waste of water, so why not plant a selection of drought-tolerant plants which can fend for themselves. Try lavender, sedum, Linum perenne, agapanthus, echinops, verbascum or sisyrinchium. Mix in plenty of organic matter while you are planting to help retain as much water as possible in the soil, then leave them to it.

HOMEGROWN DELIGHTS

Dried flowers make wonderful displays for the house and can be prominently displayed on windowsills for viewing from inside or out. How much better would they (and therefore, you) look, though, if you'd grown them yourself? For best results, choose 'everlasting' flowers such as limonium, xeranthemum and helipterum which are all annuals. Cut the flowers when they are just half open, cutting close to the bases of the stems. Tie them into bunches with string then dry them upside-down in a warm, well-ventilated place.

GAME, SET AND MATCH

Clematis produce some of the most wonderfully large and enticing flowers of all climbers. Imagine how sick they will feel next door when yours is in full resplendent bloom. Why not double that advantage by arranging a repeat performance in the autumn? Cut back early large-flowering clematis, such as 'Lasurstern', 'Nelly Moser' and 'The President' immediately after flowering to encourage further blooms. Remove about a third of the old woody stems, taking them back to about 30 cm (12 in) from the base.

UNRULY BEHAVIOUR

Like the rest of us, slugs and snails enjoy a drink from time to time, but only to be social. Use this to your advantage by making a beer trap. Set a bowl or tin can into the flowerbed with its rim level with the surface of the soil. Half-fill it with beer (they are not fussy which brand). When they drink the beer they become too inebriated to get out again, and will then drown in it. Not a bad way to go.

A PLEASANT SURPRISE

Bulbs always seem like a bonus as they pop up from nowhere, long after you've forgotten that you planted them, produce wonderful blooms in bright colours, then disappear again until the following year. Many are big enough to make quite a splash in a border – think about planting groups of alliums for their rounded flowerheads in shades of purple and pink, or tulips for a stunning late spring display. Crown imperials (*Fritillaria imperialis*) also flower in late spring and produce lovely large bell-shaped blooms in yellow or orange, arranged around a central stem with a topknot of shaggy foliage. These are impressive plants for very little work.

THE NATIONAL COLLECTION

Plant up a border with just one type of plant – all
primula species, for example, or a selection of
bearded irises – and become the local expert.
Make sure you have all their names casually
tripping off your tongue when anyone shows an
interest. If you want to take it one step further,
choose a group of really obscure plants and use
only the Latin names.

EFFORTLESS EFFICIENCY

Don't waste that space under deciduous shrubs. They may mask the
bare soil in summer when they have leaves, but take advantage of
their nakedness in the colder months with an underplanting of
cheerful spring bulbs. Choose grape hyacinths (*Muscari*), snowdrops,
crocuses or glory-of-the-snow (*Chionodoxa*) which will bask in the
spring sunshine. These little plants have evolved in woodlands where
they emerge, produce flowers and die down again before the leaves
appear on the trees and they are cast into deep shade. The bonus is
that their dying leaves will be covered by the emerging shrub foliage.

NUDITY AT NUMBER 9

Autumn crocuses (*Colchicum*) add a welcome splash of colour when
most other plants are starting to fade. Plant the bulbs in midsummer
to a depth of about 8 cm (3 in). These plants are also known as
'naked ladies' as the pink flowers appear on bare stems before the
leaves. Let it be known in your neighbourhood that you have naked
ladies in the garden and see who comes calling.

MIND THE GAP

If your flowerbeds have the odd unsightly gap, loosen the soil a little in early spring and sprinkle with some hardy annual seeds for a fantastic summer display. Choose love-in-a-mist (*Nigella*), poppies (*Papaver*), cornflowers (*Centaurea cyanus*), nasturtiums (*Tropaeolum majus*) or dazzling Californian poppies (*Eschscholzia*). Repeat the sowing a few weeks later to make sure your display lasts all summer long. After all, you are striving for perfection.

THE LONGEST-FLOWERING ROSES

It is always a disappointing time when the last rose bloom fades in midsummer, yet many will go on producing blooms if you give them a feed to boost their energy levels. After the first flush of blooms, apply a granular rose fertilizer to the soil around the plant and fork in lightly. Water well. In very dry weather, it may be better to apply a liquid feed which is sprayed straight onto the leaves, as a granular fertilizer in the soil may not dissolve. With any luck, you'll have gorgeous roses right through autumn.

SPREADING HAPPINESS

A mulch is the reluctant gardener's best friend, cutting down on two of horticulture's dullest jobs – weeding and watering. Mulches prevent weed seeds germinating, and those which do come up will be easy to pull out. It will retain moisture in the soil over the dry season, and gradually be incorporated by the worms, improving the soil condition no end. All you have to do is get a load of garden compost or well-rotted manure in early spring and spread it over your borders to a depth of about 10 cm (4 in). Simple.

BERRY TASTY

It's true to say that birds can be useful around the garden, but it is nice to encourage them just to enjoy their company, especially if they prefer your garden to everyone else's. Make them feel at home by growing some berrying trees and shrubs which will feed them when you forget to put the peanuts out. Firethorn (*Pyracantha*) has brilliant orange, red or yellow berries against evergreen foliage, the guelder rose (*Viburnum opulus*) has lovely sprays of red or yellow berries after its white flowers, while cotoneasters come in many different forms, all with plenty of usually red berries. In terms of trees, the most delicious berries seem to come from rowan (*Sorbus aucuparia*) and decorative crab apples such as *Malus* 'Golden Hornet'.

IF NEEDS MUST

If the neighbours have just planted something big and impressive, play the joker in the pack and get yourself a gunnera. This is the most enormous plant you will ever see, rather like a massive clump of rhubarb. The round leaves grow to 2 m (6 ft) across on stems 2.4 m (8 ft) high – a real giant. It needs moist soil so you will need to create a bog garden for it. Dig out an area of soil and line with black plastic or a bit of pond liner with a few holes in the bottom. Replace the soil and mix in plenty of organic matter such as garden compost or well-rotted manure. Hey presto, the biggest plant in the street.

KEEP IT CLOSE

Weeds need light to grow, so a simple way to discourage them is to arrange your plants close together. The less bare soil on offer, the less weeds you will have as the plants' foliage will literally shade them out. However, make sure your plants have enough moisture and nutrients if they are packed in tight. Well-stocked borders also look better than sparse plantings so you'll have the added advantage of a better appearance too.

STRICT REGIME

Weeding is a tedious job: one moment your borders are pristine, the next they would make a good backdrop for a Tarzan film. But how do they keep theirs so neat next door? The secret is little but often. Patrol the garden for a few minutes each evening and pull up anything you see. That way they will never get a hold. If you leave them to get well established before you step in, it will take hours of back-breaking work to clear. Which would you rather: a few minutes a day with your fingers or a long stint with a fork or spade?

TO CUT OR NOT TO CUT

Gardeners fall into two camps when it comes to deciding whether to cut their perennials back in autumn or spring. If you cut them back in autumn the borders look neat over winter, but you may miss out on some winter treats. Although the flowers and foliage are dead, some perennials have strong enough stems to stay standing through the winter and can provide some structure and interest when there's little going on elsewhere. Try the ice plant (*Sedum spectabile*), eryngiums for their spiky flowers and achilleas with their flat plate-like heads. Even though the plants will be brown, there's a certain magical quality to a winter border.

SUCCESS ON CLAY

Does your soil stay wet and sticky long after it rains? If so, you've probably got a heavy clay soil. To give plants the best possible chance of success, and to save you having to replace them later if they don't do well, add plenty of gravel or grit to the planting hole when planting, and break up the bottom as best you can. A good dose of organic matter such as garden compost, leafmould or well-rotted manure will also help to break up the clay and introduce more air into the soil.

PUT IT OFF TIL SPRING

Don't be tempted to cut back the dying leaves and flower plumes of ornamental grasses until the spring as their handsome brown foliage will add structure and interest to your garden through winter, and look especially magical when edged with frost. They also provide protection and food for birds in the hard winter months.

THE BUSHIEST FUCHSIAS

If you want the bushiest fuchsias with the most flowers (and who wouldn't?), here's how. Choose bush varieties rather than trailing types and pinch out the growing point when the plant has three sets of leaves. When new shoots develop and start to grow, pinch out the top set of leaves from each one. Continue to pinch out the growing tips of further side shoots as they develop until the plant is bushy and full. Flowers will then form on all the stems. This ensures a fantastic display of flowers, but they will be a little later than usual. Well worth the wait, though.

TOUGH AS OLD BOOTS

Every lazy gardener (go on, admit it) should find a place for some periwinkle (*Vinca major*). This wonderful plant has attractive evergreen foliage and perfect blue flowers in spring, yet it seems to thrive in the most unprepossessing places. It makes effective groundcover to suppress weeds, and also comes in a handsome variegated variety with cream-edged leaves.

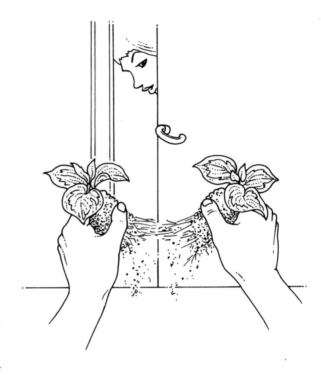

TWO FOR ONE

When you are choosing perennials at the garden centre, pick ones with more than one crown in the pot. When you get home, tip the plant out of its pot and gently pull the rootball apart into two or three pieces, each with some leaves and roots. These pieces can be planted separately and will soon grow to the size of the original plant. Plants to try include elephant's ears (*Bergenia*), hostas and daylilies (*Hemerocallis*). Keep this a secret – you don't want people to think you're a cheapskate.

THE MOST BUTTERFLIES

To ensure your butterfly bush (*Buddleja davidii*) puts on a show-stopping performance (and you get more than your fair share of butterflies), prune as early as possible in the spring. This allows the maximum time for the flowering shoots to develop on the plants, and will make sure yours is truly magnificent. As it is so vigorous, buddleja should be pruned hard. Cut back all the stems that flowered last year to within three buds of the thicker, woody stems. Aim to leave a framework 30–60 cm (1–2 ft) high.

EXTENDING THE SEASON

Autumn is a funny old time. Most of the summer flowers are over and the border plants are starting to look a bit jaded after all that hard work. Keep your borders looking better for longer by growing a few late-flowering perennials. Choose fiery chrysanthemums, dahlias, rudbeckia or red-hot pokers (*Kniphofia*). For pink or white flowers, try graceful Japanese anemones (*Anemone* x *hybrida*). Chocolate cosmos (*Cosmos atrosanguineus*), which does smell surprisingly like chocolate, also produces its velvety brown flowers at this time and makes quite a talking point.

THE MOST FLORIFEROUS ROSES

Roses cannot thrive in poor soil, so make sure you give them adequate nourishment to flower their socks off. After all, you've got your reputation to think about. After pruning each spring, sprinkle a handful of granular rose fertilizer around the base of each plant and fork it lightly into the soil. Repeat soon after flowering to help them work up to a second flush of blooms.

OFFERING SUPPORT

Many herbaceous plants start to flop by midsummer as the weight of the foliage and flowers becomes too much. This is very unsightly and leaves gaps in the flower beds. To keep your borders looking smart all season, put plant supports in place in spring. There are many proprietary plant supports available, or you can simply insert some twiggy sticks into the soil amongst the emerging foliage. For a subtle effect, make sure you do this as the plants are growing – if you leave it until the plants are already starting to fall over, you'll never get them to look natural.

THE EARLIEST HARDY ANNUALS

Hardy annual seeds can be sown straight into the flowerbed in spring, but for the earliest flowers sow in autumn. Choose old-fashioned favourites such as poppies, pot marigolds (*Calendula*) and candytuft (*Iberis*). Sprinkle the seed over a patch of bare soil, or in between other border plants. Fork over lightly to cover it with soil, then water well. The seedlings will appear soon after and by late spring they will be in full glorious flower.

THE BIGGEST CHRYSANTHS

Many people grow chrysanthemums for showing, so here's how to win first prize at the village flower show. Soon after planting the small plants, pinch out the growing tips to encourage laterals to form, which will eventually bear the flowers. When the laterals are 8 cm (3 in) long, take off all of them except just three or four. Keep feeding the plants and remove any side shoots which form on the laterals. When the buds appear at the end of each stem, snap off all but the largest bud and allow it to develop into something quite special. You will need to support chrysanthemums with canes as they will be top heavy.

LOWERING THE TONE

By midsummer some of your plants may be letting you down and lowering the tone of the border as flowers fade and plants start to look a little listless. All is not lost, however – you may get some of them to pull themselves together and flower again. When delphiniums and lupins have finished blooming, cut the flowering stems right down to the ground. At the very least this will make the border look tidier, but they may well throw up some more flowering shoots.

THE BIGGEST BLOOMS

To make your roses produce the biggest blooms in your street, nip out some of the buds as they form so the plant can channel all its energy into fewer larger flowers. Not that it's a competition of course...

BETTER BEDDING

If your bedding displays are usually a bit lanky and drawn in the shade, you are probably growing the wrong plants. Most bedding plants need a sunny spot to flower well, so pick those that are happy in the shade. Tobacco plants (*Nicotiana*) will do well, as will pansies and *Begonia semperflorens*. Busy lizzies (*Impatiens*) are perfect for shade, especially white ones which look cool and elegant. For a bit more colour, try fuchsias.

GIANT DAHLIAS

For the biggest dahlia flowers around, start by planting tubers in spring about six weeks before the lasts frosts are possible. Plant with the top of the crown about 5 cm (2 in) below the soil surface. When the shoots have grown to about 38 cm (15 in), pinch out the tips to encourage side shoots to form. Allow only 4–6 shoots to develop – pick the rest off. The main flower buds will form on the tops of the shoots; pick off any that form further down the stem to channel the energy into just one bud per stem. The blooms will be enormous.

LOOK, NO HANDS

Sprinklers and seep hoses take the time and effort out of summer watering, freeing you up to do other useful tasks such as reading the newspaper. Sprinklers shower the water over a wide area, perfect for lawns and large flowerbeds. Seep hoses, on the other hand, deliver the water in a very controlled fashion, taking it right to where it is needed most. This is more efficient and perfect for smaller areas.

WINTER WONDERLAND

Make yours the most interesting winter garden with a selection of hellebores. These delightful perennials flower from mid winter onwards. Choose the Christmas rose (*Helleborus niger*) for the earliest flowers in white, the handsome *H. foetidus* for green flowers and striking foliage, or the Lenten rose (*H. orientalis* hybrids) for large blooms in shades of red, purple, white, pink or lemon, many heavily spotted.

EAT-UP

Well-fed plants grow stronger and don't succumb to pests and diseases so easily. This will help your borders look better, but also cuts down on long-term maintenance. The easiest way is to sprinkle slow-release fertilizer granules around the plants in spring, following the manufacturer's instructions. This is really very little work for a lot of reward.

STOP THE DECLINE

It won't look too good if your borders slide into decline earlier than everyone else's, so why not give them an early autumn tidy to keep them looking good for longer? Remove dead plant debris and cut back dead flowerheads (unless you are retaining them for winter structure). Lightly fork over the soil surface to make it look fresher, and remove canes and plant supports that are no longer needed. This will make the most of the plants that are still performing well.

CHAPTER 3

AN ENVIABLE LAWN

BEAUTIFUL BANKS

Steep areas of lawn, such as banks, are difficult to mow so it is best to take a relaxed approach to the grass there. Allow it to grow long and plant with a mixture of wild flowers. It will thus become a feature in its own right rather than the land that time forgot. To ensure they will take hold, buy the wild flowers as small plants, choosing varieties that are suited to your soil and situation. Plant in the grass in the normal way, but don't add any kind of fertilizer or compost as this will make the grass grow stronger and swamp the plants. Mow the area once a year in late summer.

MOW-LESS MEADOW

Leave part of your lawn to grow long (who wants to spend time mowing?), then tell anyone who will listen that you are creating a meadow garden, an ecologically friendly area for wildlife. Who knows, it may even be true. Long grass looks good in an urban setting and you can keep a neater, closer-cropped section near the house for sitting out and children's games.

FIDDLE-FREE PLANTING

There are two ways to plant small bulbs, such as crocuses, in a lawn, both avoiding the effort of planting the fiddly little things individually. The first is to lift a square of turf with a garden spade, fork over the soil below and plant the bulbs in a group before replacing the turf. The second is to make holes in the lawn, four at a time, with a large garden fork. Push the tines well into the lawn and pull the fork backwards and forwards to widen the holes. Pop in the bulbs, pointed end up, and brush a little fine soil over the grass to fill them.

THE FINEST CUT

To achieve the most beautifully clipped lawn, invest in a cylinder mower. This will give you the finest, closest-cut bowling green of a lawn. Perfect if you plan to take up bowls, or just enjoy admiring the view from your deckchair. The blades on these mowers form a cylinder which rotates forwards and cuts the grass against a fixed blade.

DEALING WITH INTERLOPERS

When the competition's hotting up for the greenest, loveliest lawn, the last thing you will want is unsightly brown patches around the edges where your border plants have been laying on it. Keep plants in borders cut back, or use link stakes to support them. If you like the exuberant effect of plants spilling forwards, lay a line of paving slabs around the edge of the lawn. Be sure to set the slabs at the same level as the lawn so you can simply mow over the top without the need for cutting the edges.

DROUGHT RELIEF

If you decide to water your lawn in the summer to prevent it going brown, do it thoroughly as you will save water in the long run. You should aim to moisten the soil down to a level of about 10 cm (4 in) below the surface. Dig a little hole to monitor your progress. Light waterings evaporate quickly before the water even penetrates the soil and they encourage the grass to produce shallow roots, making it even more susceptible to drought in the future. If you want to save water, however, just leave it and put up with a brown lawn. Even if it has been brown for weeks, a lawn will almost always recover as soon as it rains.

LAWN LIBERATION

If you are a truly reluctant gardener who'd rather be reclining in a lounger than doing the weekly mow, why not get rid of your lawn? If it is a particularly small or heavily shaded lawn, it probably doesn't look that good anyway and will require a fair amount of effort to keep it even half decent. Pave over it, throw away the mower and liberate yourself.

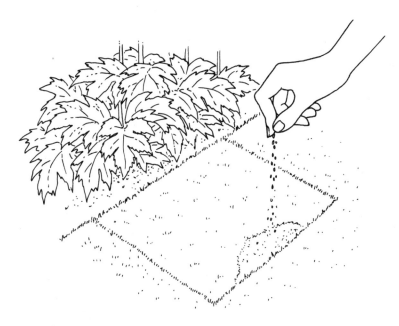

IN THE KNOW

Broken lawn edges are notoriously difficult to mend, unless you know this neat trick. Mark out a rectangle of turf which includes the broken patch of edge. Cut around the rectangle with a lawn edger or sharp knife, then lift the turf with a spade, to a depth of about 2.5 cm (1 in). Turn the piece of turf round so the edge of the lawn is now perfect and the broken patch is on the inside. Fill the broken patch with sieved soil and sow a little grass seed if it is a large hole. If it is small, the surrounding grass will soon cover it.

A STRIPE TOO FAR

Why stop at perfect vertical stripes? If you really want your lawn to attract attention, try a more pioneering approach: think about parallel curves (like a race track), diagonal stripes or even a smart chequerboard pattern made by mowing stripes first in one direction, then the other. Alternatively, cut the whole lawn with the mower blades set high, then cut out patterns in it with the blades lower. There's no end to the fun you could have with this one.

EASY-CARE LAWNS

When creating a new lawn, choose a hard-wearing grass seed mixture or turf for ease of care, drought resistance and weed suppression. These are usually known as utility grasses. It may not be as lush and perfect as a fine grass mixture but it will stay looking good if you neglect it or the children take up regular football practice in your garden.

THE STRAIGHTEST STRIPES

To achieve the perfect striped lawn, you have to have a cylinder mower with a rear roller. The heavier the roller, the more pronounced the stripes. Start by mowing a wide strip at either end of the lawn to give you space to turn. Now mow up and down the lawn in slighting overlapping stripes to make sure you don't miss any. Don't attempt this unless you are a good driver – wonky stripes look terrible.

MOWING MADE EASY

To speed up the weekly mow and cut down on the energy expended, choose a self-powered mower. Manual mowers are cheaper and lighter but you really need a powered mower if your lawn is anything but tiny. Electric mowers are cleaner and more convenient, but not as powerful as petrol-driven mowers. You also have to be close to a power supply and deal with a long cable. Petrol mowers are more suitable for tougher jobs but they are more expensive to buy and maintain.

KEEP OFF THE GRASS

Unless you want the neighbours to know exactly what you've been up to, don't walk on the lawn in frosty weather. The grass will die where you have trodden and a perfect set of footprints will appear a few days later, showing anyone who is interested exactly where you've been walking.

PEP-UP YOUR LAWN

Feeding your lawn will give it added vigour, making the grass denser and more resistant to drought in hot weather. Most lawn feeds are simple to apply: choose a liquid or granular product and apply, preferably in spring, according to the manufacturer's instructions. Many brands also include a weedkiller and mosskiller to really bring the lawn up to scratch.

AN INSTANT LAWN

If you want to lay an area of lawn but don't want to wait months for it to establish, use turf. Once the ground is prepared, turf is very quick to lay, especially if you buy the long rolls. These can simply be unrolled like carpet onto the ground. Butt them up close together and cut the turfs around the edges of the patch with a knife to get the shape you require. Water well and sprinkle sieved soil into any gaps. Keep moist to stop the turfs shrinking before the roots have grown down into the soil.

LAWN WEEDS DIE!

If the odd weed dares to show itself in your perfect lawn, there are a number of ways to deal with it. Use a pronged daisy grubber for shallow-rooted weeds like daisies and plantains. Insert it under the plant and work away gently to loosen the roots. For deeper-rooted weeds like dandelions, use a spot weedkilling gel which can be applied without disturbing the surrounding grass. For state-of-the-art weed removal, without the need for bending, try a long-handled weeder in the form of a claw or one that lifts out the weed and ejects it with a plunger. Not that you are becoming obsessive, of course.

KEEPING IT GREEN

In long, hot spells a lawn can turn brown quickly, ruining the appearance of the garden – no good for that garden party you've got arranged. Keep it greener for longer by raising the height of the mower blades. Longer grass can still look neat and it traps more dew, bringing more moisture to the roots. It is also a good idea to remove the grass box as the clippings will act as a surface mulch and trap moisture too.

SAVING TIME

Do you spend hours mowing the lawn, reversing backwards and forwards to get into all the awkward corners and difficult bits? If so, rationalise the shape. Make the lawn a simple square, rectangle or oval which you can mow in no time at all by simply walking up and down with the mower in parallel stripes. Turn the 'offcuts' into shrub borders, areas of ground cover or hard surfacing which require very little maintenance at all.

RETREAT AND REGROUP

Winter is the season in which you can relax and leave the lawn alone. If you can be bothered you could just make sure your trusty mower is in good shape. A professional service will ensure it is in tip-top condition, but at the very least have the blades sharpened so it won't cause you aggravation in the spring.

COMPOST THOSE CLIPPINGS

Every time you mow the lawn you face the same problem… what to do with the clippings. As long as your lawn is not huge, it is a realistic proposition to compost them. However, if you make a stack of grass clippings on their own it will turn into a slimy mess. You need to break up the heap with more fibrous material to help incorporate air. Either separate layers of grass clippings with alternate layers of straw, or tear old newspapers into strips and use these instead. When the pile rots down it will have turned into brown crumbly compost which you can use on beds and borders (saving you both money and the effort of driving to the garden centre to buy some).

ACCESS ALL AREAS

If access to your lawn is limited to one or two places, perhaps through a narrow gate or from a garden path, you may find the grass goes patchy around these access points due to heavy wear. Buy sheets of specially designed plastic matting which are buried into the grass to relieve some of the pressure. The grass grows through the holes in the matting to cover it, leaving a beautifully verdant patch with undercover support.

BARE NECESSITIES

If you have bare patches in the lawn caused by wear and tear, perhaps between the back door and the shed, or the patio and the washing line, you have two options. The first is to ban everyone from walking on it at all, the second (perhaps more realistic) is to lay a path across the lawn to protect the grass. Use paving slabs, gravel or bark chips, depending on the style you want to create. Whatever you decide on, make sure it has a proper edging set below the level of the lawn so you can mow over the top. You don't want to create any extra work.

A CLEAR PATH

Keep the lawn free of obstacles to cut down on mowing time. The less fiddly the job, the quicker it is – so give yourself a clear path. Avoid having island beds in the lawn which you'll only have to mow round. Banish pots and statues to the patio or stand them on plinths in borders. Keep all garden benches and other furniture on hard surfaces – if you want them on the lawn, create a small area of paving to stand them on, level with the lawn so you can simply mow over the edge. And prune back those trees and shrubs so you don't have to duck or grovel about while you are wielding the mower.

SPRING SUNSHINE

There's nothing more cheery in spring than a host of golden daffodils waving around in the grass. Many types of daffodil and narcissus are perfect for naturalising in the lawn and should go on spreading each year, gradually building up large groups. Crocuses will also grow happily in a lawn – choose the larger ones for maximum effect. And as an added bonus for the reluctant gardener, you can't mow these patches until about six weeks after the bulbs have finished flowering to allow them to build up enough energy for next year's display.

A SPECIMEN TREE

A large expanse of lawn, however velvety, can be a little featureless. Make it more beautiful with the addition of a tree. Choose one stunning subject, something relatively small with branches high enough to mow under. Be sure to choose a tree which is interesting through the year, such as the Higan cherry (*Prunus x subhirtella* 'Autumnalis'), which blossoms from autumn to spring and has a good autumn leaf colour; or the strawberry tree (*Arbutus menziesii*) which has lovely reddish peeling bark and evergreen foliage, white flowers in summer and red fruits in autumn.

EDGING SOLUTIONS

You've just mowed the lawn (it's now looking lovely), you put the mower away, and as you are heading back to the house for a cool drink and a little rest you notice the lawn edges are rather overgrown and spoil the overall effect. Strangely your energy levels seem to have dipped. A mowing strip is the answer to your problems and will mean you never have to trim the edges again. Set a line of pressure-treated timber, 10 cm (4 in) square, around the edges of the lawn, level with the surface so you can simply mow over it. An edging of bricks is also a good option but make sure you set them in mortar so the grass doesn't grow between them.

LUMPS AND BUMPS

Bumps and hollows in the lawn not only look unsightly (they result in bare patches and over-long areas after mowing), but they also offer a serious tripping hazard when you are strolling about admiring your garden, glass of wine in hand. To even them out, cut a cross in the turf right over the bump or hollow. Peel back the four corners of turf and adjust the soil level underneath, adding or taking away as necessary. Replace the turf and water well.

CHAPTER 4

THE MOST DELICIOUS EDIBLES

HEY PESTO!

Homemade pesto is definitely something to shout about. It costs a fortune to buy fresh basil in a supermarket and you need plenty for pesto, so no gourmet gardener's vegetable patch is complete without it. Sow from seed on a sunny windowsill in spring or, even easier, buy young plants from a garden centre. Keep picking out the growing tips (and eating them) as the plants grow to make them really bushy, feed and water well, and you will be rewarded with plenty of foliage for that most sublime of sauces.

EFFICIENCY AT NUMBER 8

To make the best use of limited space in a vegetable patch, try some intercropping. This involves planting a fast-maturing crop such as radishes close to a slow-maturing crop like sweetcorn. The radishes will grow up quickly and can be harvested before the sweetcorn needs the space to mature. This avoids leaving the ground bare when it could be accommodating another crop.

GORGEOUS GARNISH

As well as their invaluable and delicious foliage, chives produce lots of very pretty lilac flowers in early summer. These will transform a simple salad into something quite special, or make a wonderful garnish when you are cooking to impress. Simply buy a pot of chives from a garden centre, plant in a sunny spot and they will come up year after year with plenty of gorgeous flowers.

THE BIGGEST APPLES AND PEARS

To increase the size of your apples and pears (if you feel that sort of thing is important), you need to restrict the amount of fruit on the trees. In early summer, remove the central fruit of each cluster, plus any that are damaged or deformed, a pleasant job for an otherwise lazy afternoon. In mid-summer, thin them again to leave just one good fruit per cluster. The fruits should be spaced 15 cm (6 in) apart on the branches to achieve a really good size. Then in the evening you can stroll around the garden, tape measure in hand, waiting for the fruits to mature.

PRIZE-WINNING PRODUCE

For the longest, straightest carrots worthy of first prize at the local veg show, sow them in deep containers or raised beds of very fine, stone-free soil containing plenty of organic matter. If the soil is stony, the carrots are liable to fork and won't gain you any respect. Make sure you sow the seed very thinly and thin the seedlings to 8 cm (3 in) apart to allow them to achieve maximum size.

OOH-LA-LA

French beans are really very easy to grow, but the results can be startling. There are now varieties with brilliant yellow pods (such as 'Rocquencourt'), and even deep purple pods (like 'Purple Queen'). Tell the neighbours they are *Phaseolus vulgaris*. French beans sound so ordinary.

STRAWBERRY SUCCESS

The easiest way to grow strawberries is in containers on the patio. This allows better control over watering and feeding, and it is easier to keep an eye on anything which may be after your precious red fruits – whether it is birds, slugs or your partner.

THE EARLIEST BROAD BEANS

To win the race for the earliest broad beans, sow in late autumn or early winter the previous year. Sow the beans 4 cm (1½ in) deep, spaced 23 cm (9 in) apart in a sunny site. The seeds will germinate and the young plants will happily survive through winter. In spring, push twiggy sticks in between the seedlings to support them and keep well watered. Pick the beans (long before anyone else picks theirs, hopefully) when the pods are plump but before they go leathery.

MYSTERIOUS FORCES

Nature has some strange tricks up her sleeve. If you plant French marigold plants between your tomatoes, the plants will be protected from attack by whitefly. In fact, the marigolds attract hoverflies, which in turn feed on aphids. An easy and attractive solution to a common pest.

SLICE OF LEMON?

If you have a greenhouse or conservatory, consider growing a citrus plant, such as a lemon or orange. They make very handsome container subjects, with glossy foliage and wonderfully scented flowers, followed by fruits if you are lucky. Bring out onto the patio in the summer months and offer guests a slice of lemon in their G and T.

LONG-DISTANT RUNNERS

Runner beans are a great failproof crop for the reluctant gardener. To take the chore out of vegetables, grow them in a simple grow-bag. Lay the grow-bag on the patio against a fence and tack vertical strings to the fence as supports. Cut holes in the grow-bag and plant the seeds. Keep the compost moist and keep picking when the beans appear. There's no way you'll be able to eat them all, but weigh the beans and keep a running total – just for your own interest of course.

THE SWEETEST THING

For the ultimate taste sensation, pick peas, broad beans, asparagus, carrots and sweetcorn just minutes before you want to eat them. The sugars in these wonderful vegetables start to diminish the moment they are picked so eat them as fresh as possible for optimum flavour. You may find your peas disappear off the plants of their own accord if family members find out how delicious they are raw.

ZESTY LURE

If you are a slug, tender young lettuces and cabbages are like manna sent from heaven. Rather than spread noxious slug pellets on your edibles, trap the little devils with citrus traps. Place a number of upturned orange or grapefruit skins around the plants, then inspect them each morning and remove the molluscs you find underneath. Dispatch them in a bucket of salty water, or simply stamp on them.

MINT WITHOUT THE MISERY

Mint is invaluable in the kitchen but it does have a reputation for being a bit of a thug in the garden. Solitary confinement is the only answer. Plant mint in containers on its own, or in bottomless buckets sunk into a border to stop it rampaging. It will reward you with lots of leaves for mint sauce and boiled potatoes, and for decorating summer desserts and drinks.

THE EARLIEST RHUBARB

For the earliest, most delicate-tasting rhubarb, place a large upturned flower pot over the clump in late winter, making sure you cover the drainage hole to exclude all light. This is known as blanching. Harvest the tender, young, baby pink shoots as they emerge in spring.
Remove the pot and continue to harvest further stems as they appear.

BUNDLES OF JOY

Radishes must be the easiest edibles to grow. Simply sprinkle some seed on a patch of free-draining soil, or in a container, keep it moist and a few weeks later you will have radishes. Try a few more unusual varieties – long ones, round ones, white one, red ones, or purple ones – and tie some together in pretty bundles as gifts. You might not want to mention how easy they were to grow.

GLORIOUS GLOBES

Globe artichokes are perfect for a reluctant gardener – being perennial plants you don't have to plant them every year, they just stay in the ground and produce their mouth-watering flowerheads in late spring and early summer. These are really attractive plants, too, with huge silver leaves which stay on the plants over winter. Consider growing them in the flowerbeds along with the ornamentals. Either grow from seed in early spring or buy a plant from a nursery.

PRUNE-FREE APPLES

For extremely easy apples, try a single-stem tree. These trees are literally one single vertical stem, yet they produce a reliably good crop each year on short spurs that grow out of the stem. Grow single-stem trees in tubs on the patio or use a line of them to make a living screen. The best thing about these plants is that they don't need pruning – what could be better?

HERBS TO HAND

Herbs are trouble-free plants and many hail from Mediterranean regions so they are resistant to drought and thrive in poor soil. This makes them perfect for windowboxes. Fix a windowbox under your kitchen window and fill it with rosemary, chives, oregano, thyme and sage, all of which are obliging plants, and you can harvest a few sprigs to put in your dinner without even opening the back door.

THE CONNOISSEUR'S CHOICE

Mint is a herb garden staple, but did you know there are hundreds of varieties to choose from, each with its own distinct scent and flavour? Become a mint connoisseur and stun your neighbours with pineapple mint, ginger mint, basil mint, even eau de cologne mint, all of which smell surprisingly like their names. You could hold blind smelling competitions, but that may be taking it a bit far.

FRUITS AND FLOWERS

Courgettes are dual-purpose plants which can provide two harvests. Not only are the fruits prolific and delicious, but the fleshy golden flowers are a real delicacy. Pick off the male flowers (those without a courgette forming behind them) when they are young and fresh. Dip in batter and deep-fry, or stuff them with a meat or vegetable stuffing and steam until tender.

ALTERNATIVE ACCOMMODATION

If you don't have a lot of garden space, consider dotting a few vegetables about in your flower beds. There's no reason to have a special vegetable patch, as long as you make sure you feed them. Just about any vegetables can be happily accommodated, but some are especially ornamental and will actually enhance your borders, such as brilliantly red ruby chard, peppers and chillies, scarlet runner beans growing up a wigwam of sticks, and pretty purple French beans. This is also a great idea if you want to experiment with vegetables without anyone noticing.

SMALL BUT SWEET

If you like strawberries but don't fancy the effort of growing them, try alpine strawberries instead. These little plants will run through borders and colonise difficult patches, making quite pretty groundcover and spreading by runners. Come spring and summer, they produce lots of little ruby-red fruits. They may not be as large as normal strawberries, but the flavour is magnificently sweet and perfumed. In fact, many people mix the two varieties when eating them to improve the flavour of standard strawberries.

RHUBARB, RHUBARB

Rhubarb might have an amusing name but it is a serious proposition for the reluctant gardener. If you plant a clump now you could be picking your own flavourful stems for the next ten or fifteen years. All you have to do is feed it occasionally and pick off any flowers that appear in summer. As the clump gets bigger you should have enough stems to give away to impress the neighbours.

EASY DOES IT

Tomatoes are fussy creatures: they need very regular watering as the fruits ripen – not too little, not too much. If they are allowed to dry out, the skins become tougher, then when they do get water the fruits swell and the skins split. And because they have such a high sugar content, split tomatoes go mouldy very quickly. Water consistently and avoid periods of drought or sudden floods.

ALL SUMMER LONG

Extend your strawberry season by growing a mixture of early, mid and late-fruiting varieties, plus some perpetual-fruiting strawberries which fruit in summer and autumn, just for good measure. Perfect for one-upmanship.

KNOW YOUR ENEMY

Sow carrot seed very sparely so you don't need to do too much thinning when the little plants appear. The smell of carrots being thinned attracts carrot flies, the larvae of which will burrow into your carrots and make nasty brown tunnels. Growing onions or chives among the carrots masks the smell and this can be an effective deterrent. Another way is to do your thinning late in the evening when the flies are less active and remove the thinnings immediately. You may feel a fool gardening by torchlight but it really helps.

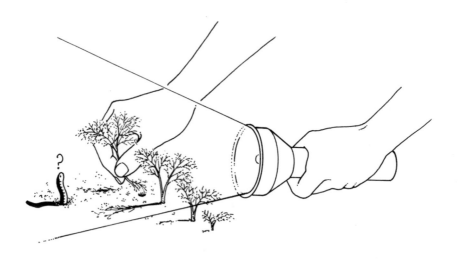

CUT-AND-COME-AGAIN

Loose leaf lettuces are perfect for growing as a cut-and-come-again crop. Sow the seed in shallow drills 8 cm (3 in) apart but do not thin the emerging seedlings. When the plants are about 15 cm (6 in) tall, cut off the tops with scissors down to about 2.5 cm (1 in). Water well and they will pop up again like magic. You should be able to do this two or three times, and you get plenty of sweet tender young leaves for your salads.

THE MOST PROLIFIC COURGETTES

To get the most possible fruits on your courgettes (is there a record for that kind of thing?), there are various steps you need to take. Courgettes are greedy plants so mix plenty of garden compost or manure into the soil when you plant them. Some people even plant them in a pocket of soil on the compost heap. They are also thirsty plants so keep the soil moist at all times and start adding a liquid feed as the fruits form. The last step is to keep picking – the more you pick the more they will produce.

FRESH HERBS IN WINTER

When everyone else's herbs have died down for the winter, wouldn't it be nice if yours were still in full leaf? There are two ways to achieve this. The first is to sow late: sow chervil, coriander and parsley in late summer and they will continue to grow through the winter on a windowsill or outside in the garden. The second is to force herbaceous herbs such as chives and mint. Lift a mature clump in early autumn, divide into smaller sections, then pot up into loam-based compost. Cut back the foliage hard and keep in a light, frost-free place. When new shoots appear, harvest regularly to maintain a supply right through winter.

THE ELEMENT OF SURPRISE

For extra cachet, grow a few unusual vegetable varieties as surprise gifts. Present your neighbours with stripy green tomatoes, purple French beans, blue potatoes or yellow courgettes. Hunt through seed catalogues in early spring to see what is available. Most of these varieties are no more difficult to grow than their more common counterparts, though yield may be a little lower.

THE QUICKEST APPLES

A juicy, rosy apple straight from the tree is a treat not to be missed. However, that may be years ahead if you are just thinking about planting now. For the quickest apples, buy trees grafted onto dwarf rootstocks as they will crop much earlier, some within four years. They are also much easier to reach for pruning and picking. If you have limited space, apples can be grown against walls and fences: choose cordon or fan-trained plants from the garden centre as they will already have been shaped for you.

CUTE AND CRUNCHY

Baby vegetables are all the rage, so why not grow some miniature carrots? They look sweet in the vegetable dish, but are also perfect as a tender and crunchy pre-dinner nibble. 'Amini' has little cylindrical roots with very little core. 'Parmex' is an early carrot with a very good flavour, while 'Pariska' has tiny globe-shaped roots.

REVOLUTIONARY RASPBERRIES

For raspberries the easy way, choose autumn-fruiting varieties such as 'Autumn Bliss'. They don't require any staking or supports and there is no complicated pruning regime – you simply cut all the stems to ground level in early spring. These varieties produce luscious fruits between August and October, a time when the season for summer raspberries is over, making them especially valuable for trading.

GROW A FEW THINGS WELL

When it comes to growing vegetables, stick to a few varieties to avoid a big workload. Vegetables need feeding, watering, picking back, earthing up and plenty of other little tasks besides. If you have just a few veggies, such as peas, potatoes and herbs, you can enjoy lots of free food for only a little effort.

TUMBLING TOMS

Even if you have only got space for a hanging basket, you can still
grow some juicy sweet tomatoes. Breeders have developed special
tumbling tomatoes with this in mind. Plants are very easy to care for
and have a spreading, trailing habit perfect for a basket. 'Tumbler' is
the best known. Line the hanging basket with polythene to prevent it
drying out too quickly and hang in a sunny, sheltered spot, against a
warm wall if possible, preferably near the back door as they need to
be fed and watered regularly to ensure a good crop of perfect fruits.

FLOATING FLOWERS

Borage is a wonderful annual herb, perfect for decorating summer
drinks with its cucumber-flavoured leaves and vivid blue edible
flowers. What could be more beautiful floating in a cocktail? Sprinkle
borage seeds in a sunny position in mid-spring and they will do the
rest themselves. These plants happily seed around and should pop up
year after year.

THE EARLIEST POTATOES

Early potatoes have the best flavour of all and are well worth
growing. Buy seed tubers in late winter – as soon as they appear in
the shops. Place the tubers in open egg boxes, one to each
compartment, and place them in a light, cool but frost-free place to
sprout. This gives them a head start and increases yield. Plant out in
early spring about 15 cm (6 in) deep, dotted about in flower beds or
in containers. By early summer the tubers can be lifted and enjoyed,
after their parade of honour of course.

THE MOST PERFECT STRAWBERRIES

To keep your developing strawberry fruits perfect and free from blemishes, cover the soil underneath the plants with straw. Do this when the fruits start to colour to keep them clean and protect them from slugs.

WHY EXERT YOURSELF?

When it comes to growing a few vegetables, don't think of it as self-sufficiency. Miss out the fiddly (and it is fair to say) most difficult part of the process and buy young plants from a garden centre rather than growing from seed. Garden centres and nurseries are stocking an increasing number of young plants as interest in vegetables grows. You should be able to get a good range of different varieties too. Look out for tomatoes, courgettes, peppers, chillies, cucumbers, aubergines, pots of runner beans, baby lettuces ready to be planted out, even pots of sweetcorn or melon plants.

PEAS FOR LONGER

Sow peas at three-weekly intervals from early spring to midsummer to ensure a continuous supply throughout the season to surprise and impress your neighbours, rather than getting them all at once. Sow them thinly in drills 5 cm (2 in) deep and support the plants with twiggy sticks.

FRESH LAID EGGS

If you really want to be top of the edibles charts in your street, how about freshly laid eggs? Hens are undemanding, require very little space, and will each produce an egg a day if you choose the right breeds. You can buy an all-in-one house and run and they need only water, grain and scraps from the kitchen. You won't need a cockerel so you won't be disturbed by crowing at dawn. And the best bit is that they are such pleasant company.

SPEEDY SPINACH

With a few minutes to spare in spring or summer and a gap or two in a border or container, sow some spinach seeds. Use a hand fork to break up the soil into a fine tilth then make a number of short parallel drills about 23 cm (9 in) apart with the side of the fork. If you sow in drills you will know which of the emerging seedlings are spinach and which weeds. Cover the seeds over and water well. A few weeks later you will have baby spinach leaves for salads, or wait and pick it when it is more mature.

LOOSE BUT LOVELY

Don't go to the supermarket for your salad leaves. For the price of one bag of leaves you could buy a packet of seed which will keep you in leaves all season. Sprinkle loose-leaf lettuce seeds in a container or patch of bare soil in a border in spring or summer and keep moist. When the plants are big enough, pick the leaves as you need them – you don't have to harvest a whole lettuce all in one go. Resow as necessary.

CHAPTER 5

CREATING STYLE EFFORTLESSLY

PARROTS BY POST?

To create style the weird and wonderful way, plant some parrot tulips. These aptly named bulbs produce extraordinary blooms with feathery edges and bizarre colour combinations, often involving green. Look in mail order catalogues put out by specialist bulb growers for the best choice. These make perfect subjects for containers where you can appreciate them at close quarters and really use the unusual colours to good effect, or plant them in an out-of-the-way patch and cut the blooms for the house.

TURNING JAPANESE

If you have a small town garden, consider going Japanese. This style is simple and cheap to implement and extremely easy to care for. Lay gravel over the majority of the garden (remembering to lay weed-suppressing fabric underneath). Carefully position a few slow-growing shrubs, such as hebes, junipers, acers and dwarf pines, ensuring the feng shui is right. Finish off with a few Japanese ornaments and maybe a simple water feature. All very stylish and very zen.

GLORIOUS GROUNDCOVER

The word groundcover usually conjures up images of dull sprawling evergreens, but it doesn't have to be that way. Annuals also make great seasonal groundcover, growing rapidly, suppressing weeds and creating a dazzling colourful display en masse. For a shady site, choose busy lizzies for their spreading growth and long flowering period; they will be literally covered with flowers. In sun, alyssum (*Lobularia maritima*) will provide dense cover and a lovely sweet scent, while Californian poppies (*Eschscholzia*) will grow quickly and bloom profusely. Climbing annuals such as nasturtiums and *Convolvulus tricolor*, with their stunning blooms, are also perfect as they will spread quickly, scrambling over the soil.

SUDDEN AND SENSATIONAL

To add colour and style to a dull vegetable patch, pop a few nasturtium seeds into the soil around the edges of the patch in spring. They will soon emerge and start scrambling around the place, with their handsome round leaves and brilliant flowers in shades of red, orange and yellow producing a wonderful show. You can even use the jolly flowers and peppery leaves to add zing to your salads. Pull the plants out when they have flowered themselves to death.

HARMONY REIGNS

Everyone loves accessories, so why not deck out your patio in satisfying colour co-ordination. Pick your favourite colour (but be realistic), and choose a barbecue, table and chairs, loungers, cushions, a parasol, garden tools and gardening gloves to fit the scheme. Colourful woodstain or paint can extend the idea and make the fences and garden shed match in. You could even get a matching bikini in case someone pops round while you are sunbathing.

ONE-UPMANSHIP MADE EASY

They have an amazing wisteria next door, laden with long lilac blooms in spring and filling the air with its soft perfume. You have to have one too. But what to buy? The key when selecting wisteria is to buy a grafted plant rather than one which has been grown from seed. Seed-raised plants take a notoriously long time to flower – many, many years – and that rather defeats the object. Just so you know, *Wisteria floribunda* 'Macrobotrys' has the longest heads of flowers, at a staggering 1 m (3 ft) in length.

SIMPLE BUT STUNNING

Garden ornaments, such as statues or even empty pots and urns, add great style to a garden and require no maintenance whatsoever.

THE NEW GREEN

Ornamental grasses, rushes and sedges couldn't be more fashionable. Seek out a specialist nursery and order something to impress. Restios, rush-like plants from South Africa and Australia, have been tipped as the new big thing. Try to track down the South African broom reed (*Elegia capensis*) or the plume rush (*Restio tetraphyllus*).

BIGGER IS BETTER

Rather than cluttering up the garden with lots of little pots, choose a smaller number of large containers instead. They will have much more impact in the overall scheme, but what's more they will take you less time to care for. You'll have to water them less frequently and the plants should be happier with more root space and less susceptible to pest and disease attacks.

DO SOME RESEARCH

Go to garden shows to find out what's hot in the plant world. You can also get some great tips in gardening magazines. Plant your new acquisition in a container so you can give it exactly the right conditions, then name drop at every opportunity. You could even host a little soirée with your new plant as the guest of honour.

START EARLY

Daffodils make a vibrant show in spring, filling the garden with sunshine. These delightful bulbs are simplicity itself to grow, but there are hundreds of wonderful types to choose from in shades in yellow, orange, red, white and even peachy-pink, some with huge trumpets and others with flatter faces. Order some unusual varieties from a bulb catalogue and pop them about in the front garden to get the rivalry started early in the year – *how* many different varieties have you got?

CREATING STYLE EFFORTLESSLY

BARBECUE BLISS

Built-in barbecues take meals al fresco to a new level. They come in all shapes and sizes, usually with the built-in chimney on top and storage area underneath. The fashion now is for a 'summer kitchen', so make your barbecue area as well-equipped as possible, then invite everyone round to admire it.

CLASSIC ELEGANCE

Not everyone has class. But a simple way to achieve it without too much effort is to plant a pair of bushy box plants in matching containers. Clip the plants into neat balls for an instant topiary effect and stand them either side of a gateway or door.

QUICK CHANGE

Plain fences and trellis can look a bit drab unless you clothe them with climbing plants, but that's just more work. Instead, paint them with a colourful woodstain for instant, eye-catching results. You may even raise a few eyebrows if you are daring enough – try red, yellow or silvery-blue.

SPOTLIT DRAMA

Garden lighting can be used to great creative effect. Nestle uplighters amongst foliage and use spotlights on statues or spiky plants for great drama. Even if you are not outside, you will have a wonderful view from indoors. And what's more, when the neighbours look out of their window after dark, all they will be able to see is your garden... looking fantastic.

SHARING YOUR SUCCESS

Boundary walls offer extra space for displaying plants, albeit of the vertical variety. Seize this opportunity to grow some delightful climbers, such as clematis and roses. If you are feeling generous you could plant scented climbers such as honeysuckle or jasmine where the perfume will waft over the fence. This is a way of sharing some of your horticultural success with your neighbours – they deserve a little pleasure now and again.

CREATING CLUSTERS

Group pots and containers together for a really enviable display. They have much more impact and are easier to maintain if they are all in one place rather than having them dotted about in the garden. The plants will be happier too as they will retain more moisture in a group as some shade others and create a more humid atmosphere around themselves. Combine a range of heights and shapes but make sure the plants work well together visually – you don't want any nasty clashes.

ARCH RIVALS

Arches make effective frames to set off focal points and vistas in a garden. Set one in a boundary or over a path to create a division and frame a view or feature. Choose from wrought iron, rustic poles, sawn timber or woven willow – whichever suits your garden style – just make sure it's the best in the near vicinity.

A GRAND ENTRANCE

Set a good impression from the outset by making your front entrance enticing. Fit an ornate gate or an arch to really set the tone. If you can't find anything you like in a garden centre, blacksmiths will make wrought iron gates to your own design remarkably cheaply – the family crest may be a good starting point. And don't forget a lock to keep out the riff-raff.

FABULOUS FOLIAGE

Don't rely on fleeting flowers to give your garden its appeal. Think foliage colour, shape and texture, which will be with you all year to ensure your garden is fabulous in every season. Choose upright spiky mahonia, low spreading junipers, and rounded hydrangeas. Mix cushions of soft silvery lavender with spiky pink phormium, yellow-edged elaeagnus with blue-green cypress. Be sure to include plenty of greens, too, to hold the scheme together and cool the whole thing down.

BIG AND BOLD

To make a bold statement in the border, plant a large easy-care grass, which will look good all year round. *Arundo donax* has blue-grey foliage up to 5 m (16 ft) high, while the pampas grass (*Cortaderia selloana*) makes a huge clump of narrow leaves up to 2.4 m (8 ft) high with fluffy white plumes. *Miscanthus sinensis* makes large vertical clumps with attractive fluffy heads. These grasses come in a variety of different colours – light green, dark green, blue-green, green with white stripes and green with yellow stripes. Grasses are extremely easy to grow and quite stunning.

SCENTING THE SCENE

Haunting evening scents are the most evocative, so make sure you've got some night-scented plants around your outside seating area to conjure up the right atmosphere for those dinners à deux. The most delicious scents are from honeysuckle (*Lonicera*), white jasmine (*Jasminum officinale*), tobacco plants (*Nicotiana*) and lilies. Plant in tubs or nearby borders and enjoy the wonderful aroma.

WATER WORLD

Large ponds can look spectacular and what many people don't realise is they don't actually require much work to maintain. For a low-maintenance option, turn over much of your garden to a large, natural pond with boardwalks around the edges and bridges over small inlets. You'd need someone else to install it in the first place, of course.

LONG DIVISION

For an informal garden divider or border edging that will establish quickly, plant a lavender hedge. These plants make a beautiful low hedge with evergreen silvery foliage and gorgeous purple flowers in summer. They thrive in dry conditions and poor soil, so you won't even have to do much to look after them.

JUNGLE FEVER

Exotic plants are all the rage, but you can create that leafy jungle effect without all the hassle of temperamental primadonnas. Choose large-leaved and architectural plants to create the right effect, just pick those that can look after themselves. To provide height and presence, choose tall bamboos such as *Arundo donax*, spiky evergreen mahonia, the large umbrella-like *Aralia elata* or colourful clumps of phormium. For sheer leaf size, combine acanthus, angelica or silvery cardoons (*Cynara cardunculus*) with red-tinged *Rheum palmatum* or rodgersia. You may want to throw in a monkey for good measure.

FLOWERING HEDGES

To make your hedges even more beautiful than they already are, train some roses through them for extra flowers with no extra effort. Plant rambling roses close to the hedge and let them scramble up through it. Blooms will appear in summer, and you can simply prune the roses along with the hedge – they don't need any special treatment.

WHITE SOPHISTICATED

If you'd like to draw on the ideas of the great gardener designers, use restricted colour schemes for your borders or bedding displays. The classic example (which sounds rather sophisticated when you casually drop it into the conversation) is the white garden. Devote a border, or even just a few containers, to white flowers and white-variegated foliage for a cool, harmonious effect. Include white tulips, white-edged hostas, phlox, roses, irises and clematis. The same idea works just as well with other colours, too.

MULCHING MADNESS

If they've just laid some gravel next door, go one better and find a more exciting mulching material. If you want something colourful, try a ground glass mulch in blue, black, white or green (recycled of course). If your style is more natural, look for stone chips in a wide range of colours, or perhaps crushed slate. You can even buy sacks of crushed shells, perfect for deterring slugs and snails. Use these mulches to cover bare soil between plants, make paths, or form a hard surface.

WINTER SHRUBS

Make your front garden the envy of the neighbourhood in the winter months with some deliciously scented shrubs. Try endearing wintersweet (*Chimonanthus praecox* 'Luteus') with its golden flowers, maroon inside; *Daphne odora* with its dainty pink or white flowers; shrubby honeysuckles such as *Lonicera fragrantissima* which have tiny cream flowers; or *Mahonia japonica* with great sprays of yellow blooms. All of these plants smell truly wonderful.

FOLLOWING FASHIONS

Bamboos are always trendy, but the trendiest of them all is the black bamboo (*Phyllostachys nigra*). This is a beautiful plant with slender canes which turn a lustrous black as they mature. And unlike other bamboos, this one isn't too rampant so you won't have to spend time trying to stop it taking over the garden. Grow in a tub on the patio or in the front garden to make sure it gets noticed.

TREASURE TROVE

You don't have to spend a fortune on garden ornaments. Found objects can be just as charming, so use your ingenuity and create a more exciting space. Almost anything will do, as long as it is attractive and it is used in the right place. Think old enamel watering cans, pieces of driftwood in interesting shapes, old garden tools, collections of shells or galvanized buckets. Become a magpie and keep a look out for treasures.

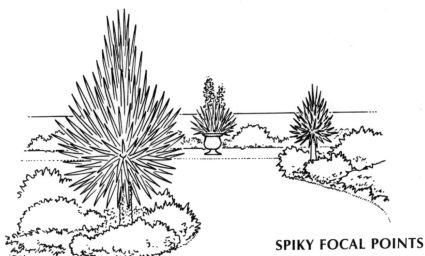

SPIKY FOCAL POINTS

Large spiky plants, such as cordyline, yucca and phormium, create eye-catching focal points and presence in a garden. Use them to provide structure in a border, or plant in containers for an instant designer look. As an added bonus, these plants are easy to care for and evergreen, so they look good all year.

FERN FASCINATION

Fern collecting was a popular obsession in the past, and once you get started with these quiet, elegant plants, you do tend to get carried away. Start a fern collection in a shady border, large container or raised bed and see how many different forms you can acquire. Landscape the border with carefully positioned rocks or pieces of log and mulch the surface with leafmould or garden compost to show the ferns to their best advantage. Then bore anyone who comes by with the intricacies of the different forms, how their leaflets are arranged, and so on.

CHAPTER 6

INSTANT FIXES

ATTENTION SEEKERS

To make your al fresco dining area look inviting, however tatty your table and chairs, place an eye-catching potted plant on the table as a centrepiece. Choose something which will flower all summer long without the need for too much attention. A bright potted pelargonium is the obvious choice for a sunny spot, perhaps a regal variety for an exotic touch or a scented pelargonium for a more subtle effect. If the table is in shade, consider a bowl of pansies, a tuberous begonia, or a busy lizzie (*Impatiens*), perhaps one of the large and floriferous New Guinea hybrids.

CATS AWAY

If next door's cat is scratching holes in your lawn, digging up your plants or leaving unmentionable gifts in your flowerbeds, now's the time to take action. There are many proprietary products on the market to repel cats and the gel-based products can be quite effective. Cats are attracted by dry bare soil, so simply watering areas where there are vulnerable plants such as young seedlings may also do the trick. This will have double the effect if you catch sight of the offending moggy when you happen to have the hose in your hand.

ALL CHANGE

Striking plants with architectural qualities stand out from their companions and really cause a stir in a mixed border, adding no end of interest. Annuals with these qualities are especially valuable as they create a whole new look which can be changed from year to year. Cleome is one such plant, sending up 1.5 m (5 ft) spires of brilliant pink or white flowers with prominent stamens, making them look rather like enormous spiders. They are simple to grow from seed, or you can buy young plants in a garden centre and pop them straight out into the border in early summer and await a magnificent display.

NO MORE BENDING

If you don't enjoy grovelling around at ground level to tend your plants, create some simple raised beds instead. This is a great idea if you are a little stiff, or simply of the opinion that bending over is undignified. Railway sleepers are the quickest option – pile them up to form a rectangle two or three sleepers deep and nail some wooden battens inside to hold them in place. This is a nice way to display small plants.

ENERGY-SAVING DEVICE

To save the trouble of walking further than is absolutely necessary, plant some herb plants close to the barbecue so you can simply reach down and pick whatever you fancy. Most do well in containers, or you can build a simple raised herb bed.

A LITTLE LUXURY

A set of garden cushions will add a touch of luxury to dining or simply lounging around outside. Choose a colour to suit your planting schemes or garden style and bring them out each evening before dinner, lovingly arranging them on the dining chairs. Rush them back inside at the first sign of rain.

GOLDFISH HEAVEN

If you don't have much space but have a penchant for goldfish, create a small but perfectly formed pond in a half barrel. Line it with butyl pond liner, fill with water and add a few aquatic plants in mesh baskets. Choose a miniature water lily, plus other non-invasive pond plants such as water hawthorn (*Aponogeton distachyos*) or the oxygenating parrot feather (*Myriophyllum aquaticum*). The barrel won't be well-insulated against the cold, so your goldfish may have to go on a winter holiday to someone else's pond.

CHEAT'S TOPIARY

Ivy is a versatile plant which lends itself to creating cheat's topiary. Make a simple three-dimensional shape out of chicken wire – a cone or ball, perhaps, or a scale model of the Eiffel Tower. Fill a container with compost and set the wire sculpture on top, anchoring it with large wire pegs inserted into the compost. Plant a few small ivy plants around the sides and they will soon grow to cover it.

FROM DULL TO DARING

For a quick fix on a dull patio, remove a few of the paving slabs, lay a little wet cement in the gaps and arrange some cobbles on top. Make sure they are level with the surface of the patio, then fill the gaps between them with more cement, pointing it neatly. Keep pets away until dry – paw prints don't add glamour.

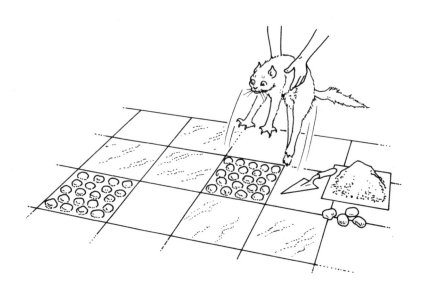

SMALL BUT PERFECTLY FORMED

Stone troughs or old porcelain sinks make great mini rock gardens to house a selection of dainty alpines. Settle a couple of small rocks into the surface of the compost and mulch with a layer of fine grit. Be sure to choose well-behaved plants as space is limited – tiny pinks (*Dianthus alpinus*), little saxifrages or *Phlox subulata* – and avoid the bullies. Place it in a sheltered, sunny position away from the worst of the wet winter weather.

THINK MEDITERRANEAN

Olive trees make stunning subjects for containers on the patio and are becoming very much in vogue. Plant as big a specimen as you can afford in a large tub, terracotta if possible, and surround with lilac pelargoniums or lavender plants to set off the silvery foliage. They are surprising hardy but won't stand the wet winter, so move to a cold but frost-free greenhouse in winter.

MAKE A MOSAIC

Add a personal touch to the garden with a small mosaic to your own design, perhaps as a threshold under a gate, or in the space created by removing a paving slab in the patio. Create a straight-sided hole about 10 cm (4 in) deep, fill it with wet cement and level the surface. Arrange pebbles of different colours, pieces of broken flower pot and tiles, or broken china and coloured glass in a simple pattern in the cement.

FASHIONABLE FEATURES

Swap your rockery for a scree bed. Rockeries are rather passé and were never going to look natural with a few rocks dotted about on a heap of soil. What's more they are a menace to maintain, with weeds popping up in all the crevices and no means of getting to them. Make a smart scree bed from a rectangle of mortared stone blocks or railway sleepers, filled with free-draining soil, topped with a layer of grit. This is more attractive, more convenient and you can refer to it as a 'scree bed', which has more cachet.

SUBLIME SCENT

Everyone loves sweet peas, especially the old-fashioned varieties which have such a magnificent scent. However, they are greedy fellows, requiring plenty of compost or manure around their roots. To avoid the need for any laborious digging, why not create a sweet pea tub for the patio? Find a large tub and put a good layer of garden compost or well-rotted manure in the bottom. Top up with a mixture of multipurpose compost and soil-based compost, to which you have added another dose of garden compost or manure. Insert a ring of canes around the edge of the tub and tie the tops together to form a wigwam. Pop in your young sweet pea plants (bought from a garden centre of course) and away they go.

AS THE MOOD TAKES YOU

Be creative with your containers, matching plants to pots for some really exciting effects. For example, plant a galvanized pot with silver-foliage plants for understated elegance, or brilliant pink pelargoniums in a pink-painted pot for a less subtle look. Don't forget the displays are temporary so anything goes.

QUICK MAKEOVER

Change your garden colours with the seasons to keep the vibe going throughout the year. As spring arrives, splash a coat of yellow paint onto flowerpots, the garden gate, a fence or a wooden bench. In summer, replace it with rich blue to create a Mediterranean backdrop to your summer borders. You will totally change the look of the garden without so much as lifting a spade.

SHOW STOPPER

To capture the essence of a wildflower meadow (without actually doing it properly), sprinkle a packet of wildflower meadow seed on a patch of bare earth in early spring and let nature take its course. You will be rewarded with a dazzlingly floriferous display of nodding poppies, dainty cornflowers and other colourful treats. Sow again the following year for a repeat performance.

PLANT A TREE, THE EASY WAY

If you would love to have a tree in your garden but the surface is paved or you simply can't face digging a large hole, grow one in a tub. Trees in tubs make great features for the patio or front garden and require very little maintenance. Choose a large container and pick a tree which will really earn its keep throughout the year. The weeping pear, *Pyrus salicifolia* 'Pendula', has wonderful silvery foliage and white flowers in spring. From the cherry family, *Prunus serrula* has white blossom in spring, followed by red fruits. The added bonus is its glossy copper bark, a great feature in winter.

NO MORE GLOOM

If you have a dark courtyard or basement garden, paint the walls or fences in a light colour to reflect more light into the space and brighten it. It is surprising what a difference this can make, and even your plants will perform better with the extra light. Choose white or cream paint or woodstain. You can take this further by choosing plants with white- or cream-variegated foliage and white flowers to really lighten things up.

LIGHTING MADE EASY

If the neighbours have just spent weeks having a state-of-the-art lighting system installed in the garden, pop to the shop and buy some solar-powered lights. You could have them in place by lunchtime. These self-contained units charge themselves up during the day and come on as it gets dark, deterring burglars and preventing you tripping over when you take the dog out before bed.

CLEVER CLEMATIS

If you have a tree in the garden, why not double its interest by growing a clematis through it, and enjoy the flowers up in the canopy in spring or summer. Choose less vigorous varieties which will not swamp the tree, such as *Clematis alpina* or *Clematis macropetala*. The showy large-flowered hybrids can also be grown in larger trees. Plant the clematis on the shady side of the tree as they like their roots to be cool and help the first few shoots into the tree using netting or wire round the trunk.

CLASSICAL CLASS

For a touch of instant class, plant a number of pencil conifers in terracotta urns and use to flank the patio or a pathway in a regular row. Choose tall, narrow varieties to really conjure up the Mediterranean: try the Italian cypress (*Cupressus sempervirens* 'Stricta') or an upright form of the common juniper (*Juniperus communis* 'Hibernica'). Combine with classical statues and stone relics and you may even believe you are on an Italian hillside.

PRIVACY PRONTO

To avoid the hours of miserable digging and ground preparation involved in planting a hedge, create a container hedge instead. Plant a row of attractive shrubs in identical containers and arrange them in a line where you require a boundary – perhaps along the edge of a path or between the back of a border and the lawn. Try box (*Buxus*), choisya, beech or lavender. Choose taller, denser shrubs if you need protection from prying eyes.

BUBBLING OVER WITH ENVY

Transform your patio in no time at all with a bubble fountain water feature in a simple kit. These kits are readily available, easy to install and look great. When the neighbours come over for a drink their envy will be soothed by the gentle murmur of moving water.

REACHING NEW HEIGHTS

You don't need a large expanse of wall or fence to grow a handsome climber. Climbing plants look great in tubs and make an interesting feature for the patio, adding height but not too much bulk. Start with a large tub, a rustic pole and a small bag of ready-mixed concrete. Stand the pole in the centre of the tub and pour the wet concrete around the pole to a depth of about 25 cm (10 in). Allow to set then fill the rest of the space in the tub with compost and plant the climber in it. Choose small plants such as small clematis varieties, white jasmine (*Jasminum officinale*) or golden hop (*Humulus lupulus* 'Aureus').

INSTANT SURFACES

The quickest and easiest hard surface to lay is gravel and it makes a sympathetic foil to the surrounding plants, looking good in just about any setting. You don't need to level the surface perfectly before laying it, but compact it as much as possible to stop it forming dips and bumps. Be sure to lay a weed-suppressing fabric down under the gravel or you will be forever weeding.

PATH-ETICALLY EASY

For a quick and easy path, get a few sacks of bark chips or crushed cocoashell. They can be laid straight onto bare ground to a depth of about 10 cm (4 in), though a layer of weed-suppressing fabric underneath will ensure no weeds can take hold. You will need to make some kind of edging to keep them in place: lay some rustic poles along the edges, held in place with wooden stakes driven into the ground either side.

POTS OF PERSONALITY

A garden should reflect its owner's personality, so express yours by customising some plain pots to your own design. Simple terracotta pots can be transformed with a coat of water-based paint in any colour you choose. Be daring – you can always paint them again next season. If the pots have moulding, pick it out in a different colour – a smear of gold paint adds classic luxury.

SOFTENING THE EDGES

To make your patio a little more agreeable, leave a few gaps between paving slabs and plant with carpeting plants. Choose low-growing, tough varieties which will suppress weeds and withstand being trodden on occasionally. Try creeping thyme, camomile, mind-your-own-business (*Soleirolia soleirolii*) or the pretty daisy-flowered *Erigeron karvinskianus*.

EMBARRASSMENT OVER

If you are bored with the sight of your patio, or frankly embarrassed by the chequerboard of yellow and pink slabs outside your back door, cover it with decking tiles which can be laid directly on top of a flat hard surface. Stain them a stylish dark green and you can start looking the neighbours in the eye again.

SWAMP SOLUTION

Got a patch of boggy ground at the end of the garden you don't know what to do with? Think of it as a blessing and plant it up with some beautiful moisture-loving plants. Hostas love it wet, as do certain ferns, irises and primulas. For a bit of drama, grow rheum with its huge red-tinged leaves. The great thing about bog gardens is they stay moist and fresh-looking throughout the summer so you won't have to water.

PLAYGROUND FUN

Most children would give their back teeth for a play area complete with climbing frame, sandpit, swinging rope and even a playhouse. Most of these can be built relatively easily and cheaply from kits. Position away from your best borders, preferably out of earshot. It should keep them happily amused for hours. Don't make it too nice, however. You don't want to attract all the other kids in the street.

COTTAGE CHARM

For an instant cottage garden feature, fill an old porcelain sink or galvanized bucket with free-draining gritty compost and plant up with sempervivums. These fleshy rosette-forming plants are very tough and happily withstand neglect. Remember your container will need some drainage holes. Mulch the top with fine grit and you have a no-maintenance feature with style.

CHAPTER 7

THE ART OF DISGUISE

COMPLETE COVER

Like all of us, trees eventually come to the end of their useful life and curl up and die. Rather than embarking on the exhausting task of digging up the stump and roots, make use of the height of the trunk by growing something pretty over it, rather like an obelisk. Tack wires around the trunk in a spiral fashion for support, then plant a clematis or climbing rose at the base of the tree and train the stems onto the wires. The dead tree trunk will soon be swathed in colourful blooms.

SMART STORAGE

If you have a small garden or very little space on your patio and couldn't possibly accommodate a full-sized shed, consider investing in a garden tidy to hide all those unattractive but essential bits and bobs. There are many different models available for storing a few garden tools, a barbecue, a watering can, some flowerpots, and perhaps a few games and toys. They are surprisingly capacious and some are even quite smart.

WASHING LINE WOES

If you feel the appearance of an empty washing line ruins your otherwise perfect garden, invest in a rotary model which can be packed away after use and stored in the shed. A rotary line also offers less risk of garrotting when you are on your way to the compost heap.

SHED MAKEOVER

There are two schools of thought when it comes to garden sheds. One is to hide it out of sight like an embarrassing relation, the other is to be proud and turn it into a daring feature. It doesn't take much work to tart up a garden shed, and there's a lot of fun to be had. Woodstains now come in just about any colour you can imagine, so pick a scheme to reflect your personality. Perhaps blue and white like a beach hut, complete with seaside motifs, or a simple stylish lilac or primrose for a contemporary approach.

THE MATURE APPROACH

To ensure your containers are always full and the displays always look mature, fill them with a mixture of permanent and temporary elements. Plant some evergreens to provide year-round structure, such as dwarf conifers, ivies and small evergreen shrubs. Supplement these each season with some colourful flowers, such as pansies in winter and primulas in spring. That way they look great every week of the year and you don't have to wait for the plants to grow or come into flower each season before they earn their keep.

DON'T BE HEAVY HANDED

If you are faced with an unwelcome view on the south side of your garden, you may not want to resort to a dense hedge or screening trees to cover it as they will block the light and cast you into deep shade. Instead pick lightweight small trees which mask the view, attracting attention away from it, but only cast a pleasing dappled shade. Birches fall into this category, with their little leaves fluttering in a gentle breeze and casting ever-changing patterns of light and shade on the lawn. The most stunning is the Himalayan birch (*Betula utilis* var. *jacquemontii*), which has lovely silver bark, a real treat in winter.

SUCCESSFUL SCREENING

An unsightly view, such as an oil tank, compost heap, or the neighbours sunbathing, can be screened from view in a number of different ways. One is to place some sort of screen in front to block the view altogether. This can be a piece of smart close-board fence, painted or stained to look attractive, or a bamboo or willow screen if you prefer the more natural approach. Another way is to plant a large shrub, carefully positioned to block the view from the area you spend most time in the garden. Choose an evergreen shrub like choisya which will act as an attractive barrier all year round and has the bonus of gorgeously scented flowers.

THREE FEATURES IN ONE

If you are clever, it is possible to adapt existing features to suit your lifestyle and avoid having to make too many exhausting changes to your garden. For example, a potentially dangerous garden pond can be transformed into a sandpit when you have young children or grandchildren (pierce some holes in the liner and fill it with play sand). The same feature can then be disguised as a lush bog garden when they grow up (replace the sand with humus-rich soil).

HI-TECH GEAR

If you really want to masquerade as a serious gardener, invest in the flashest garden tools you can afford. A ride-on mower is the ultimate acquisition, though of course you'll look silly if your lawn is the size of a postage stamp so choose a hedge trimmer or garden shredder instead. All the men in your street will be popping round to admire it.

BEAUTIFUL BOUNDARIES

Close-panel fences and trellis are perfect for instant boundaries and dividers but they can look rather new and bare when first installed. Rather than waiting for climbers to grow and soften the effect, disguise a new fence with a simple coat of coloured woodstain. There are many colours to choose for an instant design statement, from all shades of green to lilac, white, yellow or soft blue.

DIVIDE IT UP

Although it may seem counterintuitive, dividing up a small space into a number of distinct areas actually makes it seem larger. This is a great way to give a small garden a feeling of space and doesn't have to be as difficult as it seems. Plant a few shrubs to block the view right across the garden, or use a willow obelisk with a climber trained over it. A short section of fence, even a low picket fence, can also work wonders, and makes an attractive feature in its own right, perfect for supporting a few sweet peas in the summer.

THRIFTY COVER-UP

Disguise a dull garden wall by attaching a selection of wall pots. Use specially designed wall pots, which are flat on one side, or plain terracotta flower pots fixed with wire collars. Choose drought-resistant plants as small pots will dry out quickly. Thrift (*Armeria maritima*) produces handsome mounds of foliage and pink flowers in spring and doesn't require a lot of water.

COLOURFUL CAMOUFLAGE

Hide an unsightly manhole cover with a few containers of plants. Choose evergreens to provide year-round disguise and make sure they can be moved when you need access to the cover beneath. Also be sure to check the cover is secure before you stand heavy pots on it. That would be a lot of money down the drain.

GAINING SPACE

Plant the flowerbed at the end of your garden with soft silvers and blues. This will make the border appear more distant (as all pale colours do) and the garden therefore larger. Try silvery artemisia, anthemis or stachys, with blue catmint (*Nepeta*), campanulas and violas. A little visual trickery can work wonders.

NOW YOU SEE IT...

There's more to trellis than just supporting climbing plants. Use trellis panels as garden dividers to split up the space or as a light-weight screen to hide an eyesore. Because the panels are not solid, they introduce an air of mystery to the garden, offering tantalizing views of the garden beyond, at the same time partially masking them from view. Rather than laboriously digging holes for posts and mixing concrete, use metal post spikes to hold the supporting posts in position. These are simply hammered into the ground.

PLAYING WITH PROPORTION

Gardens come in all shapes and sizes. If yours is unusually long and narrow, place a large tub of brilliant red geraniums at the end of it. Bright colours always appear to be closer than they actually are, so this will make your garden seem shorter and better proportioned.

ILLUSIONS OF GRANDEUR

To greatly increase the feeling of space in a tiny garden, fix a large mirror to the wall or fence, right down to ground level so it looks like a doorway through to another part of the garden. This has a major impact. Grow climbing plants on the wall around the mirror to hide the edges and increase the illusion.

HIDE IT UNDER A BUSHEL

If your garden shed is a bit the worse for wear but you've grown attached to it, take measures to ensure it doesn't become an embarrassing eyesore. The best idea is to grow something attractive over the top. There are all sorts of handsome climbing plants: choose clematis or roses in a sunny site, honeysuckle or hops in the shade. Although you obviously want it to cover quickly, don't buy anything too vigorous or the shed will be swamped and you will be forever cutting it back.

DRAIN THEM UP THE PIPE

Drainpipes offer a bit of a problem. While you want to cover them up with attractive foliage, you don't want them to be prised off the wall with overexuberant woody stems which will eventually work their way up to the gutters and wreak havoc. The answer is to train something more lightweight over them. Choose an annual climber which dies after one season and can be replaced the following year, such as wonderful colourful morning glories (*Ipomoea*) with exotic trumpet blooms. Alternatively, pick a plant which dies back each winter of its own accord, only to reappear with fresh growth the following spring, such as golden hop (*Humulus lupulus* 'Aureus').

BORROW A VIEW

Borrow a view from outside your garden – a handsome church spire or a particularly nice tree next door perhaps – and make the most of it. Leave the view clear or even accentuate it by positioning a bench to face it or a pair of pots to frame it. Who said there is no such thing as a free lunch?

WELL APPOINTED

Position your most attractive features, such as garden ornaments and containers of colourful flowers, where they will create most impact. Maximize your efforts where you, and other people perhaps, will notice them most, such as the front garden and areas of the patio in clear view from next door.

CHAPTER 8

THINGS TO DO WITH A WINE GLASS IN YOUR HAND

DAILY VIGIL

Lily beetles are becoming more widespread, shredding lily leaves and flowers and weakening plants. The only way to protect your beloved lilies is to take matters into your own hands. Check the plants regularly and if you spot any adults (brilliant red and 8 mm (3/8 in) long), or larvae (red-brown with black heads and covered in messy black excrement), pick them off and squash them. That way they won't be tempted to come back.

TAKE A PLANT FOR A WALK

Before planting your stunning new acquisition from the garden centre, think hard about where it will look its best. Take it for a stroll around the garden and place it in various positions to try it out, leaving it there for a few days if you are not sure of the effect. Stand it next to a variety of other plants and see how they look together; sometimes unlikely combinations can look fantastic. You don't want to go to the effort of planting it and then find you want to dig it up and start all over again.

A TIDY MIND

Keeping your garden tidy is not just a matter of aesthetics and a gauge of your moral worth, but it has a practical purpose too. Piles of old flower pots, plastic sacks of rubbish and rotting vegetation can be a breeding ground for pests and diseases, so get into the habit of doing a little light tidying now and again to keep everything in order.

THINGS TO DO WITH A WINE GLASS IN YOUR HAND

A SIMPLE SWITCH

Perhaps the simplest task for early evening is to switch on your automatic watering system and relax while the work is being done for you. Choose a drip system which is economical and delivers the water right to the plant roots where you want it. These systems are perfect for containers and small borders.

GIVE THEM A HOLIDAY

Houseplants are just as decorative in your 'outdoor room' as they are in your indoor room, and add an exotic touch. Give them a holiday on your patio in the summer months – they will really benefit from the bright natural light and rainfall on their foliage. Don't forget to bring them back inside when it starts to get cooler in the autumn.

SAY IT WITH FLOWERS

One of the great joys of gardening is being able to cut your own flowers for the house. And the neighbours can hardly fail to notice your horticultural prowess if you present them with some of your triumphs in a bouquet, so take a little trip round the garden and see what you can find. If you've got a spare corner, grow some flowers especially for cutting, so you always have a supply without denuding your borders. Bulbous plants are particularly good because they usually have long stems. Try dahlias, crocosmia, gladioli, alstroemeria, tulips, irises or peonies.

TENDER AND TASTY

Radishes are among the easiest of edibles to grow. As the swelling roots start competing for space, thin them out by simply pulling up a few to allow the others to carry on growing. Rinse off the thinnings and enjoy the tender little radishes dipped in salt with your wine.

STRING UP SOME DISCS

If you have a cherry tree, you may not even know what the fruits taste like. Birds love cherries even more than humans and usually strip a tree before the fruits are even ripe. Bird scarers such as scarecrows rarely work for more than a few days as the birds soon get used to them. Instead, try CDs. Hang old CDs in the tree from strings so they can twist and turn in the breeze. As they turn, they catch the light and appear to flash. Use old computer discs or raid your husband's CD collection. If you leave the boxes in place he may not even notice they are missing.

LEARN A FOREIGN LANGUAGE

While you sit there sipping, peruse a plant directory and learn some Latin names. It is best to start with the plants you have in the garden so you will get the opportunity to drop them into the conversation frequently. As you become more fluent, choose some tongue twisters like *Matteuccia struthiopteris* or *Catalpa bignonioides* 'Aurea' to make your friends gasp.

BECOME AN ORNITHOLOGIST

Bird tables and bird feeders will encourage birds into the garden and while they are there they will forage for aphids, caterpillars and slugs, saving you a job. You also get the bonus of being able to tell everyone about all the rare birds you have seen in your garden, and how many times. No massaging the figures, though.

SAVING ENERGY

The flower power of bedding plants will be greatly increased if you remove the spent blooms as they fade. You only need one hand to pick off dead heads from your pots and containers and the display will go on much longer if the plants are not allowed to set seed.

FEED YOUR POTS

Terracotta is a lovely mellow material, especially when it has aged and developed a softening patina of mosses, algae and lichens. To speed up the process when you buy new terracotta pots, paint the outsides with a layer of yogurt (fruit or plain – they aren't fussy). This gives the algae something to grow on and takes away that brand new appearance. The perfect job for a summer's evening.

MAKING PLANS

Surely the best activities for those quiet moments with drink in hand are of the cerebral kind. As you look around the garden, think what could be better, think what you'd like to change, and think how you are going to do it. Perhaps you'd like to replace the high-maintenance lawn with some smart paving, maybe you could design a better water feature than they've got next door, maybe a few home-grown edibles would be nice. Making plans is an important part of gardening and thoroughly enjoyable, too.

INFILTRATE THE ENEMY

See what plants do well in your neighbours' gardens, then invite them round for a drink and see if you can beg a cutting or division. You will end up with plants that are perfect for the conditions on offer in your garden and you know they will do well – at least as well as theirs. And all for nothing but a bit of flattery.

STRESS RELIEF

Evening is a good time to water the garden as the plants get longer to soak up some of the moisture before it evaporates. Watering with a simple garden hose fitted to an outside tap is hardly a strenuous chore, and in fact many people find it rather relaxing after a hard day. Get an adjustable nozzle so you can turn the pressure of the jet up or down as necessary. Some have a trigger action so you can spray the water where it is needed and not when you are moving between pots or borders.

THE LEAFIEST HERBS

To get the most young fresh foliage from your herbs, pick out the growing tips from time to time. This will make the plants bush out and produce more leaves. Happily, this results in a handful of tender young sprigs which can be included in your dinner. Choose the herbs you are going to pick back depending what you've got planned for your cocktail or your meal. If you can't use them immediately, put the sprigs in a plastic bag and store in the refrigerator.

LET THEM HAVE IT

To avoid spraying chemical insecticides all round the garden, a better plan is to wash off aphid infestations with a blast from the hose, or with a bucket of soapy water. You may find this to be quite a satisfying activity.

HELP AT HAND

If you are a truly reluctant gardener, why not hire someone to do the job for you? This can either be for a one-off project or regular garden maintenance. It doesn't always come cheap, but how much is a little more free time worth to you? And think of the ripple of excitement up and down the street. Try to find someone who comes highly recommended and will answer to the name of Mellors.

NIGHT MANOEUVRES

One reliable way to control slugs and snails is to go outside after dark with a torch and prowl around the flower beds collecting them by hand. This works well after rain when they are more likely to be out and about. Dispose of them however you choose. A tried and tested method is to have a bucket of salty water to chuck them in.

BETTER BEANS

Broad beans are straightforward to grow, but the young growth is rather susceptible to attack from blackfly. When yours are in full flower, take a few minutes to pinch out the growing tips. This will remove the young growth and any blackfly with it and will also concentrate the plants' energy into the beans, making a better crop.

DO THE TWIST

Blanket weed can choke a pond, making life miserable for all the other creatures and plants in it, and frankly looking a mess. Remove it as soon as you see it. The best way is the candyfloss method. Insert a stick into the midst of it and twist so the blanket weed wraps around the stick and can be pulled out in a neat clump. Leave it on the side of the pond overnight to let any creatures which you have inadvertently caught make their way back to the pond.

BUTTERFLY SPOTTING

Butterflies and moths bring a garden to life. Take a stroll around and see how many different types you can spot, notebook in hand to keep a tally so you can boast about it later. Some garden plants attract these lovely creatures, so you may consider planting them. There's the butterfly bush (*Buddleja*) of course, ice plants (*Sedum spectabile*), lavender, achilleas and scabious.

KEEP THEM HAPPY

Like most things in life: to get something out of your vegetables you need to put something in. Feeding is an important weekly task which will ensure production rates stay high and you maintain your reputation as green-fingered vegetable expert. A concentrated liquid feed is the most convenient and can be combined with your watering routine. Follow the instructions on the packaging and make sure you don't mix it too strong or you may burn the roots. For fruiting vegetables such as tomatoes and courgettes, choose a tomato fertilizer.

DOZE IN STYLE

Every garden should have a hammock as a place for quiet contemplation, or at least dozing off after lunch. String one up between two trees, or cheat and buy a model which comes with its own frame. Climb in and enjoy.

ASSESSING THE COMPETITION

Keep a weekly check on the gardening activities of your neighbours. You need to know what you are up against. Start the surveillance with a casual walk along the road, then progress to binoculars from an upstairs window, whatever you need to do to know what they are up to.

START THEM YOUNG

If you are spending quality time with your children or grandchildren, why not pass on your gardening wisdom to them? The thing children love most is growing seeds. All you need is some small plastic pots, a bag of multipurpose compost and some large seeds, such as sunflowers. Choose a variety specially bred for its height. Plant the seeds, water well and wait for the plants to appear. Plant them out in the garden when they are large enough, then take bets as to whose will be the tallest – a bit of competition never hurt anyone.

ART OF OBSERVATION

The sooner you spot an outbreak of pests, or a disease attacking one of your plants, the sooner you can deal with it and the easier it will be to eradicate. Check your plants over regularly, looking for distorted foliage, damaged flowers, accumulations of insects or signs of distress. Investigate anything unusual and take action immediately.

THINGS TO DO WITH A WINE GLASS IN YOUR HAND

COLD BUT HOT

Chilli plants will produce bumper crops if you pick the fruits regularly. If you can't use them all up straight away, pick the ripe chillies once a week, place them in a little plastic bag and pop them in the freezer. Chillies freeze remarkably well, and defrost quickly, so you will always have fresh chillies to hand when the mood takes you for a spicy dish.

GO ON, TREAT YOURSELF

Gardening is all about planning ahead, so while you are enjoying the plants in your garden this year, it's time to start thinking about what you are going to grow next year. For a guaranteed pleasurable experience, flick through some bulb and seed catalogues and choose next season's bedding and vegetable varieties. Look for interesting new varieties, exciting colour combinations and a few impulsive must-haves for good measure. Seeds and bulbs are not expensive so you can treat yourself a little.

DO NOTHING!

The whole point of gardening is to create a pleasant environment in which to relax, a calm oasis from the busy world, your own little bit of heaven. Find a comfortable lounger (preferably with a number of soft cushions), sit back and soak up the atmosphere. You deserve a rest after all that hard work, so relax and enjoy the view.